P9-DWT-787

Dedicated first, to the people who taught me the most about China: the student teachers and leaders of the Short-Term Training Course of Southwest China at Sichuan University, 1980 and, in a special way, to the Black Fan Club — to Mary Ellen Belfiore, Sharon Hare and Sydney Hadsell, and all the other Westerners who helped a newly-arrived "Foreign Expert" teach and learn and, in a very special way, to Ian Gertsbain.

韓琳

is the stamp for "Han Lin",
Maureen Hynes' Chinese name.

Contents

Acknowledgements

This book is very much a reflection of the cooperation and support of dozens of people, some within the People's Republic of China and many here in North America.

With heartfelt thanks to my friends who encouraged me before, during and after my stay in China, and who have also given me permission to reprint and excerpt from my letters to them: to Marsha Allen, Wendy and Glenn Allen, Mary Ellen Belfiore, Michal Bodemann and Robin Ostow, Robert Byrnes, Carole Cohen, David Cooke, Janet Dawson and Doug Clark, Aline Desjardins and George Thorman, Peter Deyman and Cathy Thomson, Carolyn and Michael Egan, Michael Gasster, Sydney Hadsell, Sharon Hare, Penny Larry, Diane Mah and Ben Boer, Ian Martin, Julie and Tom Mathien, Irene McKay, Neil and Joanne Naiman, Betty and Colm O'Brien, Patricia Parsons, Nancy Peterson, Abby Pope, Nina Spada, Betty Tomlinson and Allan Anderson, and Joyce Yamomoto.

I owe a special note of thanks to my family, whom I have relied on in a way that only families can accept: to my parents, Ed and Marg Hynes; to my nephews, Michael and Kevin Hynes; to my sister, Joanne, and Rick Bolton; to my brothers, Terry and Gerry Hynes; and to my sisters-in-law, Maire Hynes, and especially to Mary Lou Souter Hynes, whose idea this book was.

And a special *xiexie* to both Michael Egan and Steve Endicott for critically reading the manuscript and offering valuable suggestions, as well as to Lorne Slotnick.

Thanks are due, also, to certain institutions in Canada: to George Brown College for allowing me to go to China, to the Canadian Department of External Affairs for sponsoring the Exchange Program to China, and to the Association of Universities and Colleges of Canada for making numerous arrangements.

And finally, to the fine and supportive collective at Women's Press, particularly Connie Guberman, Liz Martin, Lois Pike, Daphne Read, Christa Van Daele, Margie Wolfe, Carolyn Woods and most especially to my editor, Jane Springer, whose clear thinking and willingness to sacrifice sleep I greatly appreciated — many, many thanks.

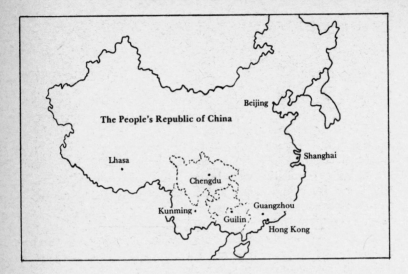

The People's Republic of China

Lhasa

Beijing

Shanghai

Chengdu

Kunming

Guilin

Guangzhou

Hong Kong

A quiet moment in Chengdu.

"Granny" doing the family laundry.

What appears to be a walking flower is really a peasant selling chicken-feather dusters.

A peasant woman selling fresh lichees in a Chengdu "free market."

Afternoon rainfall, Chengdu.

A pedicab driver in Chengdu.

A woman catches a ride home to the countryside.

Outside River-Viewing Park, Chengdu.

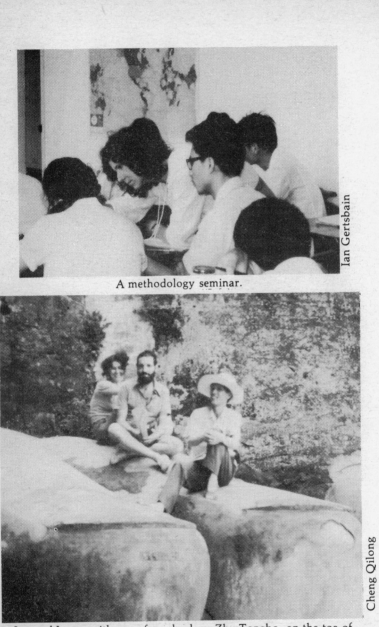

Ian Gertsbain

A methodology seminar.

Cheng Qilong

Ian and I pose with one of our leaders, Zhu Tongbo, on the toe of the Big Buddha in Leshan, Sichuan.

Sharon Hare

My final lecture for Sichuan University, on "Women in North America."

Children doing "self-study" outside one of the apartment complexes in our unit.

Sunday afternoon in a Chengdu park.

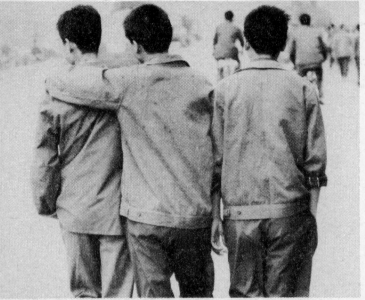

Three young city boys.

Peasant women in Kunming, Yunnan.

Ho Xinglan pauses on our way up Mount E Mei.

Age-old methods survive on the Jin Jiang River.

Pinyin

In 1979, the People's Republic of China formally adopted the Pinyin system of romanization for use in publication, and, throughout the world, most major newspapers and publishers began to comply with this standardization. Formerly familiar names and terms appeared in new spellings: the Qing Dynasty (the Ch'ing Dynasty), Beijing (Peking), the Guomindang (the Kuomintang), Guangzhou (Canton) and Mao Zedong (Mao Tse-Tung).

Pinyin is not a new system. It has been in use in Chinese schools since 1959, as part of the movement to simplify the learning of the written language; children in China now learn Pinyin before studying Chinese characters.

Once learned, Pinyin is a more accurate system for phoneticizing Chinese characters than older systems of transliteration. Because the use of Pinyin helps the English reader to approximate Chinese pronunciation more closely, it has been used in this book. One or two terms or names (Tai Chi Chuan, Chiang Kai-Shek) remain in the form they have been known in the West.

A few keys are helpful for the reader. Most vowels are given their "pure" Latin sounds, and most consonants are pronounced as in English. A guide to problematic consonants and diphthongs is included here:

Consonants:

Pinyin spelling	Chinese example	approximate English sound
c	*ci*	lo*ts*
q	*Q*ing	*ch*eese
x	*X*ian	*sh*e
z	*Z*edong	a*ds*
zh	*Zh*ou Enlai	*j*ob
ch	*Ch*onqing	pronounced as in English *ch* and *sh*,
sh	*Sh*anghai	except with the tongue curved back.

Dipthongs:

ai	Shangh*ai*	*eye*
ao	M*ao*	n*ow*
ei	B*ei*jing	*eigh*t
ie	x*ie*x*ie*	*ye*s
ou	Zh*ou* Enlai	s*ou*l
ui	Anh*ui*	w*ay*
ua	H*ua* Guofeng	w*a*ft

· INTRODUCTION ·

Tenacity and Good Fortune

March 18, 1980. So I was, finally, going to be one of the lucky ones. The phone call from Ottawa came at lunchtime to the staff room of the community college where I teach in Toronto. I had been chosen, along with a colleague and close friend, Ian Gertsbain, to teach English in China for five months.

I don't remember when I became interested in going to China, but I do clearly remember the period of my life when I got obsessed with the idea of teaching there. It had been two years earlier, and I recall precious days off that I spent trudging around the University of Toronto, trying to follow up every lead for scholarships, fellowships and postings to China. I finally found a short-term Cultural Exchange Program sponsored by the Canadian Department of External Affairs. At that time, the department was sending a team of three English teachers for three months to Guangzhou (Canton), and I submitted my application. I made it to the short list of interviewees, but was not chosen, and resolved to try again the following year. In the meantime, I set about upgrading my qualifications by giving and taking extra courses, attending conferences and presenting papers and seminars.

In the next year's competition, Ian and I applied together and fed each other's anticipation and shared each other's disappointment when we were both interviewed, but then chosen only as alternates. By the time I got to the third year, the program had changed somewhat: External Affairs was sending two Canadian teachers for a five-month period to

Chengdu, the capital of Sichuan, China's most populous province. And my feelings about getting to teach in China had also undergone a metamorphosis. The project had evolved into a simple, matter-of-fact application that I submitted yearly, like my income tax. That year I had had a gruelling winter of teaching, teacher training, coursework and my regular political work with the women's movement and my union. I was, most of all, looking forward to a quiet, restful summer, and was half-hoping that I would again be honourably turned down.

I say half-hoping. I remember friends who tried to encourage me in my third application. I dismissed their certainty that I would be accepted, and told them that I had become much less concerned because I needed a rest, not a posting to China. Throughout this whole period, I found it so difficult to believe that I would be chosen that, one day, I even walked out of a seminar on teaching English in China in order to sit in on a concurrent session on the teaching of literacy. Yet all this did not prevent me from making weekly phone calls to Ottawa to find out what stage the competition was at, or from frequently speculating with Ian on what our chances were.

The "rush" that I experienced when I got that phone call accompanied an overwhelming realization that I felt unprepared, personally, politically and professionally for a project that I had been working for years to effect in my life. Besides my perplexed delight at having accomplished such a long-anticipated goal, I was filled with panic at the number of preparatory details I would have to attend to in the month before I was to leave — from subletting my apartment to selecting and buying an adequate set of teaching materials for students about whose needs we knew very little.

In addition to the usual visa, passport and shots routine, I had to fit my packing and farewells into my regular teaching schedule and pass a final exam in a part-time Linguistics course. I found I had to delay even any preliminary learning of Chinese until after my arrival in China. For the next month, I was like a berserk barometer of human emotions, registering fear, elation, panic, smugness, desperation and uncertainty.

Getting There: Provisions and Arrangements

Compared to many other aspects of our trip to China, getting there was the least complex. Our flights and shipping costs to and from China were assumed by the Canadian government, as was a monthly salary of $750. The university to which we were sent, Sichuan University in Chengdu, assumed the costs of our lodging, food, medical expenses and transportation within China, including a ten-day tour of China at the end of our course. The university also provided us with a salary of 200 yuan a month ($120), which was modest by our standards, and modest in comparison to most other foreign teachers' salaries (usually between 400 and 600 yuan a month), but three times the salaries of most of our students. We were sent to train teachers, most of whom had at least three or four years' experience teaching English. The thirty-four students who had been selected for this "Short-term Training Course" came from universities and teachers' colleges and normal schools in the three southwestern provinces of Sichuan, Yunnan and Guizhou. They were divided into two classes of about sixteen, with four women in each class. From our experience, women were under-represented in the faculties of higher levels of the educational system although there seemed to be a fairly equal representation in the student bodies.

Ian and I were fortunate in being given accommodation on the campus, instead of in the foreigners' hotel in the centre of the city, where we had been informed we would be put up. Sichuan University, like many of China's "key" universities, was preparing itself for an onslaught of foreign teachers by building luxurious quarters, but these were not yet ready; consequently, we were installed in apartments in the teachers' housing section of the campus. We were thus initiated into the danwei, the "unit," from the outset. In the cities of China, each workplace is organized as a unit; it is the primary body of social organization and is responsible for providing essentials like accommodation, dining halls, medical facilities, and usually, social activities for its members. The unit in the cities is somewhat analogous to the commune in the countryside: it is responsible for transmitting and carrying out the directives of higher authorities (like municipal, provincial or central Party policies). Just like every Chinese citizen living in a city, Ian and I were attached to a unit, although in our case, the university was not primarily a productive unit, like a factory.

We lived, albeit with more room and with Western bathtubs and indoor toilets, surrounded by the teachers and workers of the unit and their families, as well as by our students, who were put up in dormitories. Living in the unit did not necessarily pave the way for different, or more, or better experiences, but it did bring us into close contact with the daily lives of the intellectuals and university workers. This was a view of life not easily accessible to the tourist or even the journalist in China.

Teachers and the Cultural Revolution

However constant our exposure, it was still fairly narrow. In a country of almost a billion, the number of university students is only about a million; those who have access to university education are a privileged minority at the apex of a triangle. These "intellectuals" — and our students were no exception in this regard — were quick to point out that they had had to pay dearly during the Cultural Revolution for their privileges. We heard numerous stories of schooling and teaching disrupted by the closure of the universities, of years-long stints in the countryside as "sent-down" youth, of the violence and even, in Sichuan, of the pitched battles with tanks between factions of peasants, workers and intellectuals, each claiming its own as the correct interpretation of Mao Zedong Thought. The assessment of the Cultural Revolution and Mao's part in it is a debate that still continues today, yet we consistently heard nothing but criticism of that turbulent period when the youth of the country were engaged in re-education in the countryside, or in attacking the signs of a developing class system within the Communist Party and the universities.

The fact that we heard few and grudging admissions on the soundness of the goals of the Cultural Revolution reflects not only current ideology, but also the kind of people we lived and worked with. Though we had no opportunity to investigate the attitude of the workers and peasants of China towards the Cultural Revolution, it might be expected that these sectors would be less harsh in their evaluation of that period because of the differences in their experiences during that time.

The period of the Cultural Revolution is now officially held as the years between 1966 and 1976, an extension of the period 1966-1969 to include the rule of the Gang of Four. Especially during the initial three years, the intellectuals had been labelled as one of the "suspect" classes of the population, in part because of the privileges they had traditionally enjoyed as one of the most honoured sectors of Chinese society. Mao criticized the educational system as a powerful remnant of bourgeois thought, sorely in need of restructuring. He perceived the intellectuals as capable of oppressing people by intimidating them with knowledge, and by adhering to authoritarian, feudal or Confucian methods and notions. When Mao launched the Cultural Revolution, his targets were not only the upper-level cadres and bureaucrats of the Party "taking the capitalist road" — the ones who enjoyed high salaries and who wielded enough power to maintain a host of minor privileges. He also encouraged the youth of the country to challenge and attack the "capitalist roaders" among their teachers and fellow students.

So the plight of the university teacher or student was not an easy one during the years of the Cultural Revolution: urban students were sent to remote parts of the country to receive re-education from the peasants for unspecified lengths of time that frequently stretched into years. These exiles often did not end unless a party official recommended return to the city, or until employment was arranged by the city's employment bureau — a particularly corruptible system. The universities themselves were closed for periods up to four years, and when they were reopened, many of the departments were in chaos. The regular work of the universities was cast aside as students and teachers took up full-time the political work of pursuing and maintaining the correct line of Mao Zedong Thought, an enterprise that had them putting up *dazibao* ("big character posters," perhaps better translated as "big hand-written posters"), and criticizing themselves and their colleagues publicly. In the case of the Red Guards, the youth interrupted their studies to travel around China, continuing the struggle. The whole period of the Cultural Revolution, as vivid in the minds of most Chinese as the Second World War is in the minds of those who lived through it in the West, is a fascinating and complex welter of opposing lines of struggle that never fails to spark deeply-felt reactions. Our students were amazed and sometimes amused by the extent of our interest in the period, and frequently told us that we would probably never be able to understand it fully — in fact, they were unsure they would ever understand it themselves!

"Since the Downfall of the Gang of Four..."

When we arrived in China in the spring of 1980, a new period of tremendous change was underway, a phase that dated from October 6, 1976, when the Gang of Four was arrested, a month after Mao's death. The Cultural Exchange Program we were a part of itself indicated a number of new directions. One of these was a surge of acceptance of foreign things in general, and the English language in particular. The "English fever" noted by Western journalists was definitely a fact, and the sinking of funds into salaries for foreign teachers was evidence of this. Another significant change was the renewed acceptance of intellectuals and teachers as honoured members of society, and thus as worthy recipients of such privileges as foreign newspapers, access to Voice of America and BBC broadcasts, opportunities to "study abroad" or chances to benefit from foreign expertise such as Ian's or mine.

Red Versus Expert: Who's on First?

During the Cultural Revolution, the fact that you were an expert in your field was secondary to your politics, and your eligibility for a position as a "leader" in a school, factory, hospital or commune was assessed on a political basis. Thus were the militant Red Guards able to criticize and demote, and sometimes even imprison, those professors whom they felt to be bourgeois, or Confucian, or simply ineffective in their teaching. Along with this development came a re-emergence of formerly common revolutionary practices within the units and communes; "experts" were again expected to do menial tasks — for example, doctors might be forced to sweep floors. Experts could no longer expect automatically to determine the direction of their units. There was, then, no end of mirth among my political friends in Canada who had shared with me many enthusiastic discussions about the ascendancy of the Red Guards over the experts, when we learned that my new title was to be "Foreign Expert"! Gleeful nudges would accompany the suggestion that I had abandoned my earlier "red" ways to accept the privileges and affectations of expertise in my field.

Expectations and Illusions

As I packed my suitcases and boxes of materials, I wondered what relevance my own political past would have in China. My original motivation for going to China had grown out of a general interest in communism and a concern to see it work. I agreed that the reintroduction of the "Four Modernizations" policy by Deng Xiaoping was an important attempt to bring China up to the level of developed nations in the areas of agriculture, industry, defence, and science and technology. Although I was not fully clear on how my ability to teach English would contribute to the modernization of China, I was delighted to have the opportunity to work with my Chinese colleagues in the university on this crucial task. If I was uncertain about what my contribution would be, I was even more unclear as to whether my politics in Canada would be a valuable or irrelevant background to bring to China. I felt uneasy about the "rightward turn" that China was taking internally in the renewed encouragement of some forms of free enterprise and was definitely alarmed at recent Chinese foreign policy (its friendliness towards the United States and Chile, and its invasion of Vietnam). I wondered if my stay in China would make me re-evaluate my qualified and wavering approval of the political direction the country was taking.

I was especially interested to see how my feminist concerns would be affected by my time in China. My major political work in the past had been in the Toronto Women's Liberation Movement in the early Seventies and, for the three years prior to my departure, in the International Women's Day Committee in Toronto. The example of women in China as put forward by Mao and represented by the ballets and operas of the Cultural Revolution (*The Red Detachment of Women*, *Taking Tiger Mountain by Strategy*, *The White-Haired Girl*) had been essential political input during the early days of the women's movement. I was curious to see if these images would be borne out in reality; was there really any long-standing social impetus supporting the liberation of women in China? Even in North America, Mao's powerful image, "Women hold up half the sky," had touched women's consciousness. I wondered to what extent it represented a fundamentally new outlook for women in China, or whether, like so many of Mao's sayings, it was being revamped or discarded. I wondered, too, if many of the North American women's movement concerns for personal equality and control would seem like "luxuries" in a Third World setting.

Although I did suffer a few shocks to my political sensibilities, as I did to all my other sensibilities, my experiences in China were essentially not ones of disillusionment. The things that irked and bothered Ian and me were no different from the things that have long been identified by the Chinese as problems within their system. Things like the privileges of certain cadres, the separations of families, the "poor conditions," the very long period recently when literary and cultural works were neither produced nor made available, the privileges foreigners enjoy in contrast to the Chinese — these features do not pass unnoticed by the Chinese and often touch off eloquent and witty diatribes. Even that most grinding aspect, the powerful and stifling bureaucracy that reaches into so many facets of every Chinese person's life, was a major concern to Mao, who called it "the curse of thousands of years of Chinese history."

Now that I am back in Canada and have endless chances to read and hear the reports of Western journalists from China, I am frequently disconcerted by the basic dislike many of these reporters express for the Chinese, the Party and the Chinese political system. Most of these journalists admit that the Chinese have accomplished colossal changes in pulling the country out of a chaotic, starving, feudal era in forty years. Yet many of these reporters are incapable of a fundamental sympathy or of an effort to see the experiences and problems of the Chinese through Chinese eyes. I have an antipathy for the kind of "report-card mentality" that allows many of our Western journalists to judge and grade other cultures (for example, "efficiency: poor; friendliness: excellent; consciousness about women: adequate; freedom of political expression: struggling, but healthy; overall spirit: thriving"). At the best of times, it is difficult to overcome the tendency to judge, but this kind of mentality stunts one's ability to accept China as it is, and to allow oneself to become, as much as possible, a part of it.

The "Foreign Expert"

The "foreign experts" living and working so closely with their Chinese colleagues might be expected to enjoy privileged access to the Chinese, to have an extraordinary opportunity to integrate themselves into Chinese life. Yet the special circumstances of their work often make it quite difficult, though not impossible, to experience real contact and friendships.

One problem that I had been warned about by returned "experts," and which indeed proved to be a very serious one, was that the demands and pressures of the work we were undertaking did not allow us time to assimilate and learn all that we wanted to, starting with the language. Beyond the strains of being placed in an alien culture were the ones that the Chinese agreed were heavy: being the only native speakers of an important foreign language, we were expected to do as much as we could to help everyone in the university community interested in doing so attain fluency in English. So the requests for our time came not only from our own students, but from all our colleagues in the Foreign Language Department, as well as from their students. For several hundred people, we were the sole source of new books and ideas about teaching and learning, the arbiters of grammatical correctness and the interpreters of muddy texts. We were also fascinating, if intimidating, company to spend an hour or so with. Ian and I were frequently dismayed, as we sat down to attend to an evening's marking and preparation, to hear a knock at the door that meant the next few hours would be spent helping a fellow teacher wade through a confusing morass of English prose. Whenever we bowed to the pressure to pronounce on fields outside our expertise, Ian and I privately changed our high-sounding title of "Foreign Expert" to "Foreign Charlatan"!

The Letters

The letters and diary entries that are contained here were written with an enthusiasm and faithfulness that bordered on compulsion. Each night, after our socializing, coaching and preparing for the day was done, I would stay up until one or two o'clock and pour out on paper to my friends the details of what seemed to me the strangest and richest days I'd ever had. In looking back, I am struck by how this activity was one of the few in my life that I have attacked with such whole-hearted absorption. Getting it all down was getting it all out, something that many of us in this society recognize as a precept of healthy living. It was also my only way of dealing with my culture shock, outside of talking to Ian and our fine American friends, Sharon Hare and Sydney Hadsell, who taught at the university situated beside our own. I often wrote a dozen letters a week. When all the correspondence was collected, a decision was made to remove references to the personal lives of my friends and family that would not be of interest to the general reader. Occasionally, several letters mentioned the same event, so it seemed suitable to retain, as much as possible, only one account. The redundancy that does remain in the irritations and joys I wrote home about reflects my efforts to make sense of the common details of my everyday life in China. I understand now that the whole time I was in China, I was waiting for a shedding of cumbersome layers of self, that I was irked at the padding which impeded contact and the limited possibilities for assimilation. Although I feel that I left just as this process was really beginning, this discarding and opening continues, revealing at least two very strong compulsions about my experience in China: one is to share it, and the other is to repeat it.

· GOING IN ·

It took about five days of air and train and mind travel for us to do what Hong Kong Chinese call "going in." We had a two-day stopover in Hong Kong before arriving at Sichuan University in Chengdu. The name "Sichuan" (transliterated in the new *Pinyin* system that the People's Republic has adopted, replacing the old Wade-Giles system that rendered it "Szechuan" or "Szechwan") means "four rivers." The province supports a population of staggering size, about 100 million people, or ten per cent of the total population of China. Chengdu, a city of four million, is its capital, though lesser known in the West than the larger city of Chongqing (Chungking). Besides looking forward to the fiery food, I was also looking forward to living in a province that had been open to foreigners for only a few years since the Cultural Revolution. Its location, on the Tibetan border, made it even more alluring.

Sichuan is located in the southwestern quadrant of China, and its geographical formation — it is a flat basin, ringed with mountains — has reinforced its isolation from the rest of China. In its inaccessibility, it developed as a separate kingdom that was not incorporated into the Chinese Empire until the third century BC. The poet Li Po (699-762) wrote during the Tang dynasty, "It is harder to enter Sichuan than to go to heaven," ancient words that I thought underlined my good fortune. I knew, too, that Sichuan, though very important agriculturally for China as one of its "rice bowls," has always been quite poor, and is not nearly as industrialized as the coastal regions of China.

In more recent times, Chongqing was the wartime capital of the Guomindang forces during the war against Japan, and the entire province has the reputation of being "the first province to rebel and the last to be pacified." This reputation was certainly justified during the first three years of the Cultural Revolution, when the fighting in Sichuan was especially fierce. But since the downfall of the Gang of Four, the administration of the province had been placed in the hands of Zhao Ziyang, who effected major economic changes by restoring the "three freedoms" to the peasants: the expansion of private plots, the establishment of frequent "free markets" and the controlled encouragement of free enterprise. Allowing the peasants to sell the yields of their private plots proved enormously popular, and it brought about a meteoric prosperity, both to the province and to Zhao Ziyang, who in 1981 replaced Hua Guofeng as Premier of China. Thus, with Zhao as Premier and Deng Xiaoping as Vice-Chairman of the Party, the Sichuan Connection in Beijing was assured.

Ian and I were exhausted and somewhat numb on arrival. As bewildered as I was, my mind busily got to work, trying to sort out and analyze these people and this place by describing them in my letters to my friends. Throughout my stay in China, I frequently found myself and other foreigners talking about the Chinese in a way that made me very uncomfortable. The use of the words "they" and "them" and "their" placed the Chinese in a completely "other" and undifferentiated species of humanity; yet it always seemed unavoidable when I was trying to figure out what was going on around us. And them.

After I returned to Canada, I had the good fortune to meet several very personable and friendly Chinese teachers who are now achieving their long-sought-after goal of studying abroad. One of these teachers made a chance remark that hit me with remarkable force. She described her surprise at seeing a young man take a drink from a fountain at her university in Toronto. (In China, tap water is not potable and must be boiled first; hence the omnipresent thermoses of boiled water.) She concluded he was just a kid doing a wild thing, until, a day or two later, she saw a professor do the same thing. She was then profoundly puzzled — a professor, in Chinese eyes, would obviously know what he or she was doing. She mentioned these incidents to a Chinese friend who'd been here a year, and the friend replied, "Yes! They drink cold water!"

Here were a couple of Chinese in North America doing exactly the same thing that Ian and I, and hundreds of other foreigners, had done and were doing in China: absorbing and accounting for "their" strange customs by observing a series of random daily events. Perhaps it was naive of me never to have considered that this process might be mutual, but I was nevertheless gratified to see a Chinese person going through the same perplexing experience of trying to explain foreigners to herself.

But I am jumping well ahead of myself: within a day of our arrival, we had to start the task at hand, the teaching. The class list of our "trainees" materialized in front of us, sitting in pairs in three rows of desks in adjoining classrooms. Our students were neither undergraduates nor graduate students; most of them had graduated from university three or four years earlier and had been teaching English since then in various colleges and universities in the three provinces of Sichuan, Yunnan and Guizhou that make up southwest China. They ranged in age from their mid-twenties to their early fifties, but most were, like us, in their early thirties. Only nine were teaching in institutions in Chengdu, and the rest suffered quite badly from homesickness and found their return to the dormitory lives of students less than comfortable. They had been selected for the "Short-term Training Course of Southwest China" on the basis of recommendations made by their own department leaders and had been given an English proficiency test to determine their standing. The results of this examination, along with preliminary interviews that we conducted, helped us place them in the higher or lower of the two classes.

Within the first few days of beginning our classes, it became apparent that our students were experiencing as much difficulty as we were adjusting to the new situation. One of my students wrote of experiencing "a gulf of shyness" that he had to conquer simply to speak to me. For our students, coming into contact with a Westerner was an unusual and intimidating experience: they were afraid of our finding their English inadequate as well as the unfamiliar experience of having a foreigner at the front of the room speaking so quickly and effortlessly. It was essential for us to find ways to ease our students through the period when they, too, were experiencing a form of culture shock.

The fact that most of our trainees came from outside Sichuan University and were in a special teacher training course that interrupted their regular careers had the effect of isolating us from the rest of the faculty of the Foreign Language Department. Unlike many "experts" teaching in China, Ian and I were not placed in teaching groups with Chinese teachers giving the standard courses of the university. All over China, in the sixteen "key" universities, short-term training courses of five months were being set up for English teachers and were run by "foreign experts" who were given complete freedom in determining course content. It seemed to us that those experts who had English teaching experience in Canada, the United States, Britain or Australia were assigned teacher training; and the experts from the same countries who had no teaching experience, or who had taught subjects unrelated to English, were given undergraduate English courses to teach, with the same freedom in selecting course materials and methods. In China, as in many Third World countries, the mere fact of being a native speaker of English often qualifies an individual as an English teacher.

So our special status as foreigners was underlined — our job was to teach our thirty-four students. In addition, anyone who wanted the privilege of access to us could arrange this through elaborate channels of permission that we did not understand and had no control over. The leaders and department heads felt the opportunity of access to native speakers was something that had to be shared, yet controlled, as much as possible.

Throughout our stay in China, we were constantly asked one well-memorized formula of interaction, "Have you gotten accustomed to the life here?" We always answered that we had; but in truth, there were a great many things that it took a long time to get used to. My first letter, begun on our first day in Chengdu, reflects on the shocks we were undergoing as we settled into life at Sichuan University: shocks over the language, the conditions and the poverty, the staring and the questioning, and the appalling amount of hard work ahead of us. For me, the letters served as shock absorbers.

Sunday night, April 27, 1980
Arrived today in Chengdu
Well, Janet,

This is an extraordinary, overwhelming, staggering experience. First of all the flight has totally worn us out, but we're in excellent spirits, nonetheless. Second of all, despite my, ahem, political awareness, I was not at all prepared for the extensive poverty. Third, the "foreign experts" are so isolated from each other and other people that I can already feel myself becoming quite aggressive in dealing with these obstacles. Fourth, they expect an awful lot of work from us. We have to meet with the "Group Personnel" (bigshots) tomorrow at 8:30 to decide our schedules, so we'll see how that goes.

Oh, where to begin? Ian and I have flats in a complex on campus; his is on the third floor and mine's on the first. We have no kitchen or hot water, though we have a gas burner/hotplate for heating water. It hasn't been necessary for me to figure out how to use it yet since thermoses of hot water are provided daily.

Living at the university is like living in a village. Everyone and their families lives on campus, so there's washing hung out on bamboo poles everywhere. A small store or two, a barbershop, a bath-house are some of the amenities we've noticed and used. The laundry facilities are flat marble slabs with a cold water tap, outside all of the complexes. When you picture this, imagine it a thousand times more "primitive." Don't like that word, but it's accurate.

There are two things that are absolutely wonderful about this place. One is the food (delicious beyond my wildest expectations) and the other is the unreal friendliness of the people who can speak English. The other people just stare. We are the first Westerners they've *ever* seen; Ian's beard must be like a burning bush; even the hair on his arms is something the children want to touch. I get the feeling that if I offered to show them the inside of my purse or even my shoes they'd be crawling all over me. People almost have accidents on their bicycles craning their necks behind them to look at us. It never stops.

This letter has been written over two or three days. Don't have time to write it all at one sitting. Breakfast is at 7:30, lunch at noon, dinner at 6 o'clock. We go to the "canteen," two large buildings with an open courtyard between them. When we arrive, people — many, many of them — are there, picking up squares of rice or *mantou* (steamed whole wheat bread — delicious) in aluminum boxes or enamel bowls. The rice is not completely polished, which is the way I like it. The crowds stare at us, from their bicycles or standing around on foot, eating their meals (some/most take it back home). We go into a bare concrete, under-construction building, and at one end is a room that has a screen and some nice tables and stools. And then, after we've picked our plates and spoons and bowls and chopsticks out of the basin of hot water and dried them off, enormous masses of wonderful hot spicy meat and vegetable dishes are brought to us, along with soup and rice and noodles and *mantou* and once we had fried potatoes! Miss Li, my guide-interpreter, who is impossibly formal most of the time, has offered to teach us how to cook.

Imagine meeting a former student on the street in Toronto: stilted conversation. All our conversations are like this, except we are often interrupted in the middle of explaining something or answering a question with things like, "What is the best way to learn a language?" "What is your age?" (When I hedge on that, they assume I don't understand and press further.) "Do students in your country have a lot of opportunity to talk to foreigners?" "Are you married to him?" (meaning Ian). No, we smile, we're not a couple — just friends. I have the feeling we're going to be answering that question a lot in the next five months.

Not an hour goes by without one of us thinking and verbalizing how lucky we are to be here together, and, on top of that, to be friends. Ian and I have been getting along wonderfully; in fact, so far, with less difficulty than any of the friends I've ever travelled with. He's really a hit with the kids. He's going to write a letter to Elaine saying, "Look around you, right now, wherever you are. Whatever is there *is not* here." It's hilarious, but it's true: no curtains (they're coming), no fridge, no ice cubes, no well, no *anything*. Ian says he would kill for a J-cloth. But the people who are looking after us are so generous. We have only to mention a need (and sometimes they just perceive it) and it appears. The need for the J-cloth comes from the fact that the place is, ah, not too clean.

Ian has just come in and told me he has found out from another foreign guest, an American doing research here, that there is *a* washing machine here at the university. It's in the Physics building. Where else would you put *one* washing machine?

The abovementioned American, Michael Gasster, is an extremely nice man who thoroughly knows the ropes and helps us out immensely by translating our delight to the cooks (and by telling them we don't need so much food). This morning at breakfast he told us the woman who serves us wanted to know our names, and that it was best for us to have Chinese names, and that he'd been thinking of good Chinese surnames for us, and that a Chinese person could give us first names later. He suggested "Guo" for Ian (the name of a Sichuan liberation hero) and "Han" for me (an old, old established name, meaning, in fact, "Chinese"; Han Suyin's surname). This is the kind of gentle, thoughtful person he is. He's selling Ian his son's bicycle (his 20-year-old son was here but has left) and we're going to buy another one for me, at the Friendship Store (for foreigners only — another way one is segregated). The guides were adamant that I buy a medium-sized bicycle, but I've held out and am getting a large one.

The bicycle will be an enormous boon, since we feel slightly imprisoned on campus. It's far from the central core here, and when we get the bikes we can *explore*. We have no real sense of where we are. Michael has given us a map of the city in Chinese and marked some places of interest (the Western-style "coffee shop" — coffee! — the hotel, which has a bar and wretched food, the museum).

The scenery is beautiful, the city and the campus impoverished, the campus particularly so since it's undergoing an incredible amount of reconstruction — since 1977, the overthrow of the four you-know-who's. The university looks like it was almost totally demolished during the Cultural Revolution. I haven't wanted to take too many pictures for fear of drawing a crowd. (Why do I care? We draw a crowd anyway.)

The weather is lovely, though damp. It's still like early spring — warm afternoons, chilly evenings, though insert a British Isles dampness into this. Even this paper is dampish as I write on it.

I think we'll be happy here. One thing is clear — the amount of work we'll have to do is enormous. They expect tons out of us. So much for getting some time before we started in to work; they had us giving a lecture to the faculty the day after we arrived, one to the students today, and one to our own students, the "trainees," tomorrow. There are some frustrations; the main one is not knowing any Chinese. We've asked for language lessons, but who knows?

When the Chinese don't like an idea, they change the subject, and that's what they did when we pressed this "request." And although the workload will be heavy, I don't think it will be beyond our capabilities — which was a major fear.

When we gave our lectures today, to the entire student body of the English Department, about 150 of them (on "Student Life in Canada" — we chose the topics), I was amazed at my own unconcern. I drew up some point-form notes about an hour before I did it, spoke for about a half an hour (and so did Ian) and then we entertained questions, of the inevitable type: "Do many people in Canada believe in God?" "Do you?"

I've given you no idea of how we got here, I guess because the present surroundings are taking all our attention. Landing in Hong Kong and staying there for two days seems like a century ago. It's an amazing city, all glitz, neon and consumerism. We whirlwinded our way through there; I bought (gulp!) $300 worth of camera equipment for my Minolta — and Ian bought (what else?) a watch. We spent another fortune on stuff for teaching (tapes, batteries, head cleaners, anything we could lay our hands on). The proprietors of the stores encouraged us to buy staggering quantities of things "before you go in." This ominous expression stuck in my mind. It made it seem so irrevocable. Do we ever talk of "going in" to any other country?

We were so flustered and frightened the day we left Hong Kong. In our haste and frazzled states of mind, I managed to leave my jeans and a jacket in the hotel room (getting them back delayed us quite a bit) and Ian left his suit hanging over a railing in the train station (a briefer delay). Finally we got on the train, and the ride into China actually began. "Now the cars turn into bicycles," commented a British woman sitting beside us.

We were met by two people from the Guangzhou Ministry of Education — we, being the only two foreigners who appeared at quite a loss, were fairly easy for them to identify. They guided us through Customs, and as we straggled down a walkway out of the train station, someone jumped out and took a picture of us! It turned out to be Mary Ellen Belfiore, that friend of mine from Toronto who's teaching in Guangzhou. She hastily made arrangements to come and visit us that night before we were whisked off in our car to our hotel.

The hotel was spooky. It was like an empty, luxurious, cavernous movie set. Mary Ellen later told us it was the hotel that Nixon had stayed in. She brought two other women, "experts" also, that night, and Ian and I opened our duty-free booze to celebrate the occasion. We all talked compulsively till 10 o'clock, when the taxis stop running.

The next morning, oh, so early, the same two Chinese took us off to the airport to catch our flight to Chengdu. We were in the air for only about an hour — in the first-class section with high-level cadres and such — and really didn't have enough time to adjust to the fact that our journey was ending.

At Chengdu airport, we were met by what seemed like dozens of people, though in retrospect, there were probably only seven or eight. Ian and I were plunked into separate cars (I can't tell you how wrenching that was!) for our trip into the university, and this is how we met our interpreters. Miss Li, my interpreter, introduced me to my car-mates, and Jiang, Ian's interpreter was, I suppose, doing the same in his car. There was polite talk of Norman Bethune, and then we arrived at the university. "This is where we'll be living?" I inquired tentatively. "Of course," said Miss Li. (You'll remember that telegram we got in Toronto saying we'd be put up in the hotel in town.)

So this is how we got where we are now.

DIARY ENTRY
Friday, May 2

Ian sits in one of the gold corduroy armchairs,
painstakingly rewinding our one excellent tape, *The
Manhattan Transfer*, which we listened to once before my
tape recorder pleated it. The Voice of America veers in
and out of the airwaves; this is the first time we've been
able to pull it in — the 9 o'clock news, accompanied by a
high-pitched whistle and static from the Vatican. We've
taken our evening stroll around the campus, and drew a
crowd when we stopped to look at the photo essay on Liu
Shaoqi, "who was criticized during the Cultural
Revolution." We met a woman from the Foreign Affairs
Department who took us on a tour of the swimming pool.
In total darkness, it was a little hard to admire or assess.
Ian's interpreter, Jiang, has dropped in, and tells us the
"gas station" is open from:

6 to 8 in the morning
11:30 to 1 in the afternoon
6 to 9 in the evening

so this is when we can turn on the gas to heat water on
our hotplates. But the gas station is "out of order," as is
my hotplate, so...

And then ensues a two-way language lesson; Jiang is
learning /l/ and /n/ distinction and production, because
he says things like "afterloon," and we are practising our
numbers and learning how to tell time in Chinese. Jiang
seems like such a nice person — he's delighted to spend
relaxed evenings with us, just chatting. Although he's the
interpreter assigned to Ian, he's a teacher here at Sichuan
University (as is Miss Li, my interpreter) and is also a
student in my class.

Saturday night, May 3
Dear Penny,

Have been thinking of writing you a letter all day, and what a day it's been! I'm not sure if we're over our jet lag or not, but we've been exhausted ever since we arrived. And it's one whirlwind day after another, as Ian says.

Today we had a meeting with the department honchos ("leadership cadre") and they made clear their intentions to wring us dry. Here, for example, is our schedule:

1. teaching: 8 to 11:30 Monday to Friday

2. lectures: one two-hour lecture every other week (to the whole department), Monday afternoon

3. "tutorials":   two afternoons a week. This is scheduled individual sessions with our trainees, Tuesday and Thursday

4. meetings: one meeting one afternoon a week (Wednesday) with all the teachers in the department — we give information on latest teaching techniques

5. "committee":   one meeting once every other week with the leadership cadre

6. films: one film plus discussions every week or every other week. This item unsettled!

7. field trips: Saturday or Sunday afternoon, sometimes (with the whole class)

And they've been acting like they're doing us a big favour by letting us not teach on Saturday morning. Oh, *groan*.

We're also going a full 20 weeks and not getting out a minute early (September 12) and there are no breaks scheduled.

But rest assured that Ian and I are bearing up well despite these grim prospects. "The living standard" as our students constantly point out, is not what we're accustomed to (did you know the average wage in China is $163 yearly?) and Ian is coping amazingly well. Even to his own surprise. It's astounding to see him become frugal; saving bits of string, empty cigarette packages and beer bottles, old plastic bags. He's thrilled with each new improvisation, for example, his new rug on the floor beside his bed (a plastic laundry bag ripped off from the Hong Kong Hilton — we picked those rooms dry of all their freebies against such times as these, and how wise we were). And of course as much as we're making do with all this, we are living in the lap of luxury, with even a sit-down toilet in our flats, instead of a squatter.

Write me a brief note and tell me what to talk about. It's all incredible. I can't choose.

I suppose the thing I was least prepared for was the staring. It's absolutely unnerving. Children gaze at us open-mouthed, parents stare flatly, young girls giggle and old women walk up beside us and inspect. The thing we can't do is stop while we're walking — anywhere, on campus, on the street, in parks, in stores. If we stop, say to chat with someone who's said, "Good afternoon" (English words!), a crowd gathers. Ian and I lay bets on how many will gather. It's always at least ten, sometimes close to 30. And if we turn and say *ni hao* ("How are you?") everyone falls apart in astonishment.

There's an incredibly nice American, Michael Gasster from Rutgers, doing history research here — another expert — who speaks Chinese, and who has been *very* kind, explaining the ropes to us. He made a neat comparison about how the Chinese react when we speak to them during one of these marathon stares: "It's like talking statues."

If it weren't for Michael, we'd be lost. He gives us all the news he gets in Chinese and that's "kept" from us. Like how the swimming pool opened for the season yesterday. The reason we hadn't been told, he explained, is that the Chinese are afraid we'll drown or at least harm ourselves. He's given us a map of the city, explained how to get the Voice of America (known among experts and students as "the VOA," please) on our shortwave, told us the one place in the city to get coffee, taught us a few essential phrases (like "peanut" so that I could inform the kitchen staff of my deadly allergy) and generally been very supportive.

It's a blessing to have someone like him around because we are kept so isolated from everyone. We were whisked into the city (far) in a car with curtains on the windows, no less, to do some shopping in the Friendship Store (towels, slippers, glasses) and then to a handicraft shop, where we bought some very beautiful batiks. "Impulsive buying," said Miss Li, my interpreter. She's one of our students, and the only one who wants to be called "Miss," even though we've told her it's sort of odd for someone who's married. Another comrade, a very nice one, is going to give us Chinese lessons. *And* we are getting bicycles this week! That will mean real liberation. Again, we've been warned 75 thousand times about the danger of riding bikes. The city *is* horrendously busy with bicycles, but we desperately need them.

I've said next to nothing about our students. They're wonderful. So warm and appreciative and admiring. But so demanding! They want linguistics, phonology, how to *write* a poem in English and recite one, not to mention methodology! great literature, feature-length films, reading, writing, speaking, listening and, dear God, "free conversation." They have the most careful English imaginable. At least ten times a day we're told not to "stand on ceremony." When you finally manage to teach them a more appropriate phrase, they overuse it till you

want to strangle them. This happened with "Let's go" —
an attempted substitute for "We must be off now."

Well, dearie, I must be off.

May 4
Dear Michael and Kevin,

We haven't been to the zoo yet, but we did see some
pandas on a program on the colour TV on the train (!)
coming into China. The countryside is very poor and the
people have to work very hard. We are living in
apartments at the university and our meals are cooked
specially for us. The food is wonderful! Everyone is very,
very friendly and is very happy when we try to speak
Chinese. We're learning slowly. Did you notice my first
Chinese characters on this card? They say "Canada." And
may I remind you of your promise to write your poor
stranded auntie to tell her who wins the Stanley Cup?

Sunday, May 4
Dear Mom and Dad,

Well, here's the letter you've been waiting for. I knew
you'd be worried, so I asked the people here to send a
telegram the day we arrived. I think they thought it was
hilarious, or at least inexplicable, that I'd want to send
you a telegram on arrival.

As I explained in the postcard, Ian and I have been
given flats in a professor's residence. They are very nicely
furnished with new furniture (bamboo chairs, big
armchairs, a nice desk, two attractive dressers, an iron
bedstead, beautiful quilts, fluorescent lights, terrazzo

floors). At first we didn't have curtains and mirrors, but we've scrounged them. So we're all set. There's no hot water, but we have hotplates and kettles to heat it. The food is absolutely superb and the quantity is overwhelming.

We are getting bicycles next week, and our official language lessons (*our* Chinese lessons) are starting on Wednesday. Once we have our bikes and can manage our way with a tiny bit of the language, we'll feel a lot freer. As it is, we are completely dependent on our guides, which is okay since they're so generous with their time, but what we would *really* like is to feel able to navigate around ourselves. The campus is quite far from the city core, and just last night we learned how to take a bus into town. That was an adventure and we felt like accomplished voyageurs when we'd managed it! The city is beautiful.

Our hosts have been incredibly kind. A wonderful banquet was put on for us at the hotel downtown, with many, many lavish courses and plenty of beer, wine and "strong spirits." We were guests of the president of the university and he gave several moving toasts to the friendship between Canada and China, and to us.

Our students, as well, are very, very nice. They're hard-working and expect a lot of both us and themselves. The months ahead are definitely going to be plenty of work.

Our materials, not from Canada, but from the other institute in Guangzhou (Canton), arrived yesterday, so in addition to all the books we lugged transoceanically, we have these books, and a duplicating machine. Which means we're fairly well-equipped until our own fortune in books arrives. That's a relief.

We've figured out the money system, an elementary accomplishment that is compounded by the fact that there are *two* currencies, one for the Chinese and one for foreigners. "Foreign currency" is new; it's only been around for a year or so, and is in the same denominations as regular money. It's what you can get in exchange for your dollars, but it can be used only in Friendship Stores.

We are paid in Chinese money (200 *yuan* a month, about $120) by the department. The basic unit, like the dollar, is the *yuan* (or ¥) which is worth about two-thirds of an American dollar (66¢). The *yuan* is then subdivided into tenths, called *jiao* (or *mao*), which are worth about 6¢; and the *jiao* is then divided into *fen*, worth an infinitesimal amount — one tenth of 6¢. So, since it's a decimal system, it's fairly easy to understand.

The weather has been lovely. Mild, warm spring-like, though it's damp like Ireland. But not at all chilly and none of the heat yet that I was afraid of. We had a brief rainstorm for half an hour yesterday, when it rained like hell. But it was over quickly.

Tuesday, May 6
Dear Mary Ellen,

A treat, getting your letter! One of the first to arrive. I'll never forget the feeling of peering at you as I was coming down the ramp at the train station on our first day in China. Ian and I felt so lost and bewildered and the whole journey was taking so long that it was beginning to seem unreal. It was a thrill to see a familiar face. That evening with you and Wendy and Nina in Guangzhou was just what I needed, and believe me, your words have rung in our ears, guiding much of what we do. Especially in our so-called "negotiations."

The wring-em-dry approach is being carried to extremes in our case: they had us giving lectures *the day after* we arrived, and the following two days. The constant admonition to "Have a good rest" — which we have become sickeningly familiar with, exactly as Wendy predicted — while they load on the work. Hmph. We didn't so much have a round of banquets as a round of plays and ballets (even May Day was no exception) during which we kept dozing off! So we *began* exhausted and are still coping that way. What's peculiar, I think, is that the more onerous the task, the less formally it's dumped on us. For example, walking out the door, someone will say, "Oh, by the way, at tomorrow's meeting, you'll give a lecture — just an hour or so — on language learning, all right?" Freak out. Our solution is to agree, and say, leave the topic up to us, and then to do a thing on describing the set-up of Western TESL (Teaching English as a Second Language) teacher-training courses or some other such minutiae.

We're not staying in a hotel, much to our surprise. We have *flats* on the campus, in a professor's residence. I wish like hell we'd been able to have a look around at Guangzhou, especially your institute, because we have nothing to compare this with, so it's all a shock. Living here is like living in a village, remote from the city centre, complete with chickens and our own gas supply. We have no hot water, natch, but gas heaters (a hotplate, I mean — losing control of the language here). Mine only works when there's someone around, checking out my complaints about it. Ian's toilet does the same routine.

The fabulous food we get makes up for everything. This is one of the reasons I hope you get to visit us. It would be wonderful. I'll start working on it from this end. You could always sleep here, in my flat, because I have a spare room that is locked up and used for storage. It might be like moving mountains to have them open it up, but we'll see. And as for the food — *five* people couldn't eat the amount they serve us. We're not going back to Canada skinny, I can tell you that!

Tomorrow our official Chinese lessons start — this is something we negotiated for and they really couldn't refuse since we're doing, it seems to me, about twice the courseload of everyone else. And we're also getting bicycles, so that the foreign-experts-whisked-to-the-city-in-curtained-cars shackles will soon be lifted. I suppose the custom of putting curtains on car windows is a hangover from the days of sedan chairs? Any idea?

We're lucky to have an American expert around; he's doing research here and eats with us (the only other one). He is constantly being asked to explain the Nature of Chinese Reality. "Must ask Michael about that" is as common a saying on our lips as "Have a good rest" is on everybody else's.

Well, it's two in the afternoon, alarm clocks are ringing out of all the windows around me, and we have to get back to the department for "office hours." Although Chengdu is quite a beautiful city (I think — but as I said, I have nothing to compare it with) I'm glad we're not living downtown. Makes life a lot easier.

Oh, heavens, how could I have forgotten! The materials and the duplicating machine arrived on Saturday, to our enormous relief.

Yes, it is a good feeling to know we're in this together, and you *must* try to get here in July. There are Tibetan people in the streets of Chengdu. We can stare at *them*. Take care.

Some postscripts later that evening:

Just spoke to a honcho about "my Canadian friend teaching at Guangzhou who has some holidays in July" — could she come and visit? "Work?" he replied (one-track mind), "No, visit." "Ah, for two or three days?" "Yes." "Ah, could be possible, uh, ah." The groundwork is being laid.

On reading over this letter, realized how it seems a little snarky about the people here. You also know how incredibly kind and generous some individuals can be. The comrade who's giving us our Chinese lessons, for example. It's just that so much is so puzzling and so many reactions are unfathomable. And I haven't said anything about our students. Everything you prepared us for is true here, too. Emphasis on textual analysis, painfully formal English, the touchy difficulty of trying to wean them from political clichés. All this after a few days' teaching. I'm trying to do as many activities as possible that will make them react in English instantly instead of planning each statement for 20 minutes beforehand. It's killing them. And the stilted conversations are what's gonna kill us.

Thursday, May 8
Dear Carolyn and Michael,

I'm sitting up late in bed, very tired, but rebelling against all the work I have to do. Our teaching has begun, after several days of giving lectures to various groups and interviewing our students. I think they think we're superhuman. We also had a round of plays and ballets to attend, but we were so exhausted and the performances so unfathomable that the distinguished foreign experts kept dozing off. One startling moment in the "ballet" was the singing of an "American song" in Chinese: "Jingle Bells." On May Day.

Neither May Day nor May 4 was formally celebrated, except for people clogging the parks and streets and for foreign experts being whisked to ballets. It was explained that the Chinese people can no longer afford the expense of the celebrations. There are a couple of things that are probably different from living in Beijing or Guangzhou — Chengdu is supposedly architecturally quite different from most of China — many of the buildings have half-timbering. It's quite beautiful, but very poor, and very industrialized. I probably have never lived in such a polluted atmosphere — with even a (gulp) nuclear plant on the campus. Don't tell my parents. You see the occasional Tibetan on the streets, but they are not the centre of attention. We are. We cannot *ever* stop, anywhere — on campus, on the street, in a store — without a crowd gathering, staring at us in disbelief. At first I was really unnerved, but now, when I see a Westerner, I do the same thing.

Miss Li, our prim and proper interpreter (unlike the male one we also have, Comrade Jiang) has offered to give us Sichuan cooking lessons. We wormed Chinese lessons out of the honchos, and a wonderfully nice person, Comrade Li, gave us our first lesson tonight. *When* will I be able to hear the tones? It's killing me. About all I can manage is to yell *ni hau* ("How are you?") at the stares; and *xiexie* ("Thank you") and "Good-bye" and "beer" and "very good" and "allergic to peanuts." My one sentence: "I am a Canadian teacher at Sichuan University." And I have some numbers. But I can't negotiate in stores yet. I have a mental block about this language.

But it's not necessary to negotiate in stores. First of all, there aren't any on the university grounds. Secondly, when we go to stores, it's with the interpreters, who take over to an incredible degree. The campus is far from the centre of the city, and neither of us has learned how to get around in Chengdu, since we're whisked downtown in a curtained car. Our interpreters are inexperienced in many things we consider basic. They had never, till they met us:

- mailed an airmail letter out of China;
- been to a bank;
- made a long-distance call;
- sent a telegram;
- and, of course, spoken to any more than three or four Westerners. Oops, I tell a lie. Miss Li's husband was the interpreter for Trudeau when he was in Chengdu last year. *He* went to Lhasa, Tibet; and we've asked to go, too. This is going to be interesting, to see how they handle that request. This is for our tour at the end.

This cocooned-within-the-university-grounds feeling is soon to end, because we're getting bicycles this week! "Foreign Experts Take Off," read the Chengdu dailies' headlines!

A couple of things are saving our sanity. One is a sense of humour. I hope we're able to maintain this. Many ridiculous things happen, or inexplicable things, and we simply guffaw (as discreetly as possible) — the Jingle Bells incident is a good example. The other sanity-saver is the presence of one other expert. Michael bucks us up in moments of irritation, gently explains why we're getting so indignant, tells us hilarious stories and generally keeps us informed. And he doesn't stare. He also does a lot of translating for us.

Our students are amazingly friendly, though freaked out by our teaching methods. The most wearing aspect of the next five months will be the endless stretch of kind intentions and formal conversations. Don't be surprised if I come back speaking with an upper-class British accent, saying things like "Are you there?" to answer the telephone, and simultaneously using a spittoon. What an experience this is.

May 8
Dear David,

You've probably gotten my postcard about dropping a line to Lao Gui; now, it's not necessary to send it, because the materials from Guangzhou arrived on Saturday, including the duplicator. The problem is, now we're stuck for stencils and fluid. We didn't bring these with us because Peter Mitchell, the former Cultural Attaché at the Canadian Embassy, swore up and down that they would come with the machine. Anyway, we fortuitously ran into him in the Friendship Store, because he was leading a tour there, and he says the Embassy will be able to do something about it. Mary Ellen Belfiore said she can pick some up in Hong Kong and send them to us. So we're working on both these angles.

Our students seem to have started out with the kind of openness that I think you were experiencing with your group at the end of the course. This is due, I think, to the current political atmosphere, which permits them to air their grievances about how held back they were from professional progress during the Cultural Revolution ("My English books were burned by the cadres and peasants"). Does this sound familiar from your stint here two years ago? But, my, they're demanding, and it's not just them — one disadvantage of living on campus is that all kinds of people are forever dropping in, textbooks in hand, wanting explanations of each line of a book they'll have to teach or study in the fall. As I'm sure you know...

Li Guolin, your former student, has been exceedingly kind and solicitous; he's the one who helped us take our one and only independent trip to the city — he put us on a bus. And then worried till he saw us the next day. He's going to take us into town on Sunday, and give us a tour of one area of the centre (an appealing itinerary — three restaurants, two parks, a temple, several stores).

We had a splendid evening with Nina Spada, Wendy Allen and Mary Ellen Belfiore the night we arrived in China. They appreciated the contact with home and Mary Ellen was thrilled to see a familiar face (as I was!). They regaled us with hilarious stories, warned us about overwork, formal British accents, reading aloud, The Turners (a British set of tapes that are ridiculously la-di-da); we opened our duty-free Kahlua and talked about Canada. And they encouraged us.

Since then I've heard from Mary Ellen that she has a break starting July 10th and she's going to try and visit us then. I have clearance from this end for her to stay here. I'm already looking forward to seeing her...

DIARY ENTRY
Thursday, May 8

Two momentous developments: first of all, yesterday I'd broken down and admitted that I actually was sick; the allergy that was scaring the hell out of me turned out to be not that, but a full-blown miserable cold, fever, cough, snot. So I reluctantly agreed, during our first Chinese lesson last night, to see a doctor, and I chose to see a herbal medicine doctor rather than one who practises Western medicine. Jiang's wife dropped in with him during our Chinese lesson and, as she is a doctor, was able to diagnose the cause as "changeable weather" — which, along with the Cultural Revolution, is the culprit responsible for all personal and social evils.

Really, the cause is exhaustion. Today, the appointment duly made, Miss Li marched me off to the Chinese medicine doctor in the clinic on campus. I sat in a big wicker chair at the doctor's desk, while another doctor sat at an adjoining desk, attending to a line-up of people. My doctor, a woman, took my pulse throughout my little interview (this is the time-honoured method of diagnosis in Chinese medicine), never once looking at a watch. She got up and came back with two large paper bags of herbs and two smaller plastic packages. When I got home, I looked inside the bags and was startled (and sickened) to see cicada corpses in the one I have to start tomorrow. Miss Li took them home and boiled up today's remedy — it's bitter, but palatable. She got impatient with me swallowing it in a series of gulps, with gasps in between, rather than pouring it evenly down my throat, which I was constitutionally incapable of doing.

The tea was not the only thing she brought with her; she also summoned Ian for our "instructions" from the head of the Foreign Affairs Department on campus, the people officially in charge of us. They are as follows: we are not to go off campus without telling her or Jiang where we're going; we are not to go off campus after dark.

So our wild fling on Saturday night when we got Li Guolin to put us on the bus into town and our subsequent return in a taxi at 10:30 did not go unnoticed. Rather it touched off shock waves of alarm, and special new rules have to be made up for the contingency of the experts going off campus. Miss Li said that we were the responsibility of Sichuan University, and that they always had to know where we were (of course, we don't know where they live, so how could we find them to tell them we're going out?). She said that if any harm should come to us that she and Jiang would be "criticized" and "punished." Ian promptly blew up, bless him. They both argued fiercely about these new conditions, and she insisted we comply. Finally, much to our surprise, Miss Li allowed that she had done her part, informing us of our instructions, and that we would now have to "negotiate." That's what the Foreign Affairs Bureau chief said would have to happen "if we said 'no' " — so at the end of the argument we discovered that they were expecting us to refuse! Ian got Miss Li to agree she might feel as angry as we did under the same circumstances. Me, I was ready to agree to all of it and then disregard it; I didn't want to jeopardize getting our bikes, which is an event scheduled for tomorrow.

DIARY ENTRY
Friday, May 9

Michael's reaction to the above scene: first of all, he'd never heard of such conditions being imposed on foreign teachers; and secondly, he reckoned they were just putting themselves "on the record" as having warned us; and thirdly, he was betting that that was the last of it, and they wouldn't come back to us about the problem [which is precisely what happened].

May 10
Dear Betty and Colm — and Emer and Maeve,

That news clipping you sent from *The Globe and Mail* was the first and only time we heard that Beijing has now prohibited the showing of foreign films in language classes. (What a peculiar case, too — the ban supposedly coming into effect because of that adolescent who murdered someone in Beijing after watching a lot of foreign films.) I wonder how long it'll be in effect, or if it's seen as permanent. Sichuan University seems to be out of the mainstream, that is, in the "boonies," and consequently the higher-ups haven't heard about this new ruling (and I'm not about to tell them) — to such an extent that they're begging us to provide them with National Film Board films. And that rests on the good graces of the Canadian Embassy in Beijing. I can just predict what's going to happen: the Canadian Embassy will comply with the Beijing ban, but none of the leaders here will ever hear of it.

The music tape is getting plenty of air time in our flats here, and the Buddy Holly "Maybe Baby" cut turned out to be the first classroom song. The students could define rock and roll as "American music popular with young people" but had never actually heard any. The state of music is amazing here: on May Day we were taken to a "ballet" (actually a variety show, ending with a piece from *Swan Lake*). Ever since that performance, when we heard "Jingle Bells" in Chinese, our students have been begging us to teach them the English words. They cannot understand that it's a song we sing in only one season. The other disconcerting thing about performances here is that no one applauds. More news to come.

Thursday, May 15
Dear Mom and Dad,

Well, life here is getting into a routine, which is a relief, in a way. We've got almost two solid weeks of teaching behind us — it's a grind, lots to do, and plenty of extras, but the students themselves make it all worthwhile. They're incredibly friendly and concerned and are always "mothering" us to take care of our health, be careful on our bikes and all. And they're so hardworking.

Yes, we have got our bikes — magnificently heavy black Chinese models with very sturdy bells that are absolutely necessary. The ringing of bells is constant — as is the honking of horns. It's a good thing the ratio of cars to bicycles is approximately opposite to the ratio in Canada — otherwise we'd be deaf by now! The roads are full of bicycles with the occasional car and a few more trucks. But we're spared all the noise and congestion, living at the university.

Our boxes arrived today! But typical of the "reddest of red tape," as Ian calls it, we can't pick them up at the train station till the receipt mailed from the Embassy in Beijing gets here. Argh. Anyway, that's pretty good time. Soon we'll be all set.

There's nothing we really need here — you might want to clip the occasional article from the paper and slip it in with your letters. We're able to get the Voice of America and the BBC on our shortwave here, so we do get some news. We're especially interested to hear what happens with the referendum in Quebec. And you could remind people to write; even the odd postcard is an event! I haven't started craving anything yet, although I occasionally dream about a glass of white wine. But I'm satisfied because the beer is excellent!

May 15
Dear Penny,

Thanks one hundred million times for your letter. Ian and I read it over lunch six times, laughing and tsking over each bit of news. Glad to hear the union is soaring from success to success and the songs of victory are in the air — this is the way our students write — and that you fought the good fight.

You've got our schedule — which actually has been lightened, thank God. We ride over to the department — takes five minutes — and plop down for quick cups of tea in our adjoining offices which are rooms 212! [incredibly, the same room number at the office we all share at George Brown College] and 214. Then we go up to class and face our students. Ian has the "A" class (16 students) and I have the "B" class (18 students). Their standing was determined by their TOEFL (Test of English as a Foreign Language) marks. There are only four women in each class. They come from three different provinces: Sichuan, Guizhou and Yunnan; ages 26 to 51. A pot-pourri of backgrounds, but many of the young ones were admitted to university after the Cultural Revolution with very little high school training. The people in my class have a lot of trouble understanding natural speech. My remark: "Look, there's some people on the roof"; their reply, "Yes, the children in the day care are very noisy this time of day.") Their writing's not very good, and it has the same problem as their speaking: an addiction to formulas, clichés, inappropriate collocations ("Excuse me, I have to go now, I have other fish to fry.") This, by the way, is one of the things that makes us laugh. But it also drives us crazy. They don't say anything without planning it for ten minutes. Ian has been pouncing on the people in his class for this kind of stuff, but things are a little more complex in my class. My people desperately need their confidence built up. They will not ask any questions in class. The only saving grace is they throw themselves heart and soul (a common cliché here) into anything I assign them, including speaking activities.

They know exactly how they want to be taught, and are very resistant to/sceptical of anything else, despite their avowed hunger to be exposed to "new" methods. They want to read, read, read and then have us analyze the text paragraph by paragraph, summarizing each, explaining "background" (culture!), vocabulary, grammar. They don't want to answer questions on the text, they want to hear us explain it. B-O-R-I-N-G! Not to mention the violation that's being done to the teacher/student-talk concept! Ah well, it's an uphill struggle, not because any of the content is difficult to teach, but because they are so addicted to this textual analysis approach. This is one of the things that irritates us. One of the leadership cadre is a slavedriver. That irritates us as well. You know, always asking you to do enormous tasks in what seems to be no time, like taping three TOEFL tests on a "free" afternoon.

And you asked about things that make us laugh and cry. Nothing has made me cry, though plenty baffles and puzzles me. Our exceedingly correct interpreter, Miss Li, mothers us to bits (zips up my purse, takes money out of my hands to pay for my stamps). She's one of Ian's students. She seems to have *no* sense of humour, while Jiang, our other interpreter (one of my students), who is much less proficient in English, loves to go along with our gags. Our simple-minded jokes. He says things like "I foolishly forgot to pick up your laundry today." He's a dear, though he doesn't seem to have the "connections" Miss Li does. When I found out Miss Li's husband had gone to Thailand (he's an interpreter), I tried to invite them to eat dinner with us. She replied, "Well, I eat at 6:30 and you eat at 6." "We could change that," we ventured. "Well, your place is so far from mine that it really wouldn't be convenient." (She *doesn't* live far away.) So we left it. Later I told Michael about this incident, which I thought staggeringly rude. He said, "Well, it just shows you how reluctant they are to do that kind of thing. It's better to take them out to a restaurant. They enjoy that more, anyway. It's more of a treat." And indeed, that's what she had proposed as an alternative. Miss Li has no idea how harsh she sounds. Ian once mislaid a tape (a student picked it up by mistake) and she told him in front of the class, "You are a *very* careless man." I was horrified, but Ian was amused.

Now, for something that pleases me. That's hard. I think what will please me the most will be acquiring some degree of ease and familiarity with this culture. I don't expect a lot. Just some. And it will be pleasant to get to know this city. And it will be pleasant to be able to manoeuvre a bit in the language. It's so *hard*! Just as my mental block about Chinese was softening, I learned that, *in addition to tones*, Chinese has *stress*. My mind snapped. Our Chinese lessons are given by a wonderful comrade, Li Xingui, but our progress is slow. We're learning the pronunciation, and a few basic sentences: "I am a teacher. I teach English. I work Sichuan University half year." I cannot master the tones. Tone deaf.

Our very, very best to you, devoted friend of the distinguished foreign experts.

韓琳

May 17 — a rainy Saturday afternoon
Dear Janet and Doug (and Oliver if he can take the time away from his tap dancing lessons to read this),

What a delight to get your note, and the picture of you and Oliver was an unexpected pleasure. I opened your letter at one of the breaks, with all the students crowding around (as they always do) and showed them the picture. They went nuts — with curiosity, that is. The first serious question here is always "How old are you?"; so that was

asked, along with husband's occupation, "Boy or girl?",
in that order. One woman student was so touched by the
picture (it reminded her of her own five-month old in
another city — a lot of students come from other
provinces) that it brought tears to her eyes. Me, when I'm
so far away from anything familiar, I stop believing on
some level that home exists; and so it was a shock to see
your living-room!

Ian wrote in a letter to Penny that he's going to start a
Foreign Charlatans' (as opposed to Foreign Experts')
Club. He's been asked to give a lecture on the
Demography of Canada to the newly-formed
Demography and Population Department, as well as to
teach French to one of the honchos here.

Whew! The first week we were teaching, my notorious
clumsiness brought about the first lucky break we've had
here. We were still bone-tired from the flight (and I
suppose just the shock was wearing us out). Anyway, one
morning as this gent was accompanying us up the stairs,
I, in my usual graceless fashion, tripped and spilled all my
books. Much concern on his part and much embarrassment on my part. Little did I realize the consequences:
later that day, the honchos had a meeting with Ian and
me, and they asked us if we were tired. Feeling very
overworked, I said, "Yes, a little." "And you were giddy
this morning?" (he meant dizzy). I was perplexed, but
then the department head raced on to offer us a four-hour
a week reduction. We took it gratefully, and only later
figured out the connection. Ian has promised to take me
to dinner at the Courtyard [a Toronto restaurant] in
gratitude for my clumsiness. I blame it on (credit it to) my
Birckenstocks.

The students are charming and considerate and almost
devoted, on the one hand. On the other, they very
forthrightly demand detailed analyses of the texts we use
in class. Still, they are cooperative and love games and
role-plays. But oh! how they write: "Since the smashing
of the Gang of Four, the songs of success have been

echoing in the air, and news of victory pours in from every quarter." Where to begin?

I guess the only thing I miss is a sense of familiarity, in some quarter or other. I wrote you, I think, about all the staring and crowd-gathering that occurs whenever we step out of our flats. It was amazing at first, then unnerving; now I feel irritated, and want to tell people not to be so rude. Except, now — whenever *we* see a Westerner, we're flabbergasted, too!

Well — take care of yourselves. There is a big memorial ceremony for Liu Shaoqi this afternoon on TV and I want to go over to the department to puzzle over it.

DIARY ENTRY
Monday, May 19

Yesterday, Michael took us on a bicycle ride in the countryside to see a waterwheel that he'd spotted last week. He was intrigued by it because he'd never seen one in China before. This was an especially interesting one: it was made entirely of bamboo and was functioning perfectly, irrigating the nearby rice paddies. We rode out in the awful heat and then walked our bikes on the mud paths between the paddies, up to our ankles in mud and up to our nostrils in fertilizer-sewage smell. Peasant women were engaged in the back-breaking labour of transplanting rice seedlings by hand into the paddies.

I took some pictures of the waterwheel, and that attracted a bit of attention. One woman wanted me to take some pictures of her kids, and so I did — after she had peeled about six layers of clothes off each of them, to get down to the cleanest ones, I suppose. It made me even hotter just looking at the amount of clothing those kids had on. I promised to mail them some prints of the pictures, so an older man wrote their address on an old cigarette package.

We said goodbye, got ourselves and our shiny new bikes a little muddier and rode down the road a bit further. We decided we had to turn around when we came to a sign that said, "No foreigners beyond this point" in Chinese, Russian and English. Michael had also promised to take us to a place that intrigued us as much as the waterwheel had him; this was a "Western-style coffee shop" he's been talking about. "Well, what do you say about pushing on to the Café Vienna?" he suggested, making up on the spot the most unlikely name it could possible have — but hitting on our fantasies quite accurately.

The Café Vienna, as it shall now be called, is a fine place. It was crammed with the Sunday afternoon family crowd, consuming ice cream, pastries, orange drinks and the iced coffee which inspired its new name (and which, unfortunately, did not look very appetizing). Michael stood in line to get ice cream, but came back with drinks. "Every time I come here, they have just run out of ice cream," he said with some chagrin. I didn't mind. I was so thirsty I had two orange drinks.

韓琳

Tuesday, May 20 — oui ou non?
Dear Marsha,

Your letter was "warmly welcomed" as the Chinese (always) say here. My constant companion, Yonny [Ian], battles daily with his students, the top class, about their overuse of clichés. "A tough nut to crack" is how one of his students described him. *My* class is an even tougher nut to crack: their reading is at advanced level, their grammar fine, but everything else varies. They are friendly but shy but demanding but retiring. Hmm. A real mix. In every way.

Glad to hear the usual round of outings, plays, dinners and drink-ups continue in our absence. Did you get our telegram for your birthday? It was fun sending it. We did it from the hotel in town, a haven where Westerners are not surrounded and stared at every time they stop. People in the hotel are more accustomed to weird-looking people in bright clothes, so we get only passing, furtive glances there. (Mauve shoes like your new ones would just about put people in hospital from bicycle collisions due to craning necks.)

Please say it isn't so about a possible mail strike. Life is difficult enough.

What I mean by difficult, before you get alarmed, is that it's so difficult to get anything accomplished here. Buying toilet paper, for example. When you go back to the store that had a shelf full yesterday you find that today it's out. Ian has developed a habit of buying anything he thinks he might need when he sees it. (This is a new development? you ask yourself.) Ah, but what's different is that what we're buying are things like tea, candles (sometimes the electricity goes off), matches, cigarettes, glue and soap. We have to restrain ourselves — buying two rolls of toilet paper is looked askance at. And here's the full text of a letter from the Canadian Embassy, received yesterday: "Dear Ms. Hynes, Attached is a receipt you will require to pick up the teaching materials that have been sent from Beijing to Sichuan University yesterday by slow train. Sincerely, etc." The materials arrived last Thursday, but our Chinese comrades know their way around the bright red tape so they managed to get the stuff without the receipt.

薛琳

Wednesday, May 21
Dear Mom and Dad,

Well, we are both curious about what was happening in our home and native land all day today, and tonight interrupted our Chinese lesson to pull in the Voice of America news broadcast at 9 p.m. (9 a.m. your time) and heard about the 60% *non* and 40% *oui* in Quebec. Ian was surprised, I was disappointed, but that's another story.

The money end of things here has been holding out well; just as you predicted, expenses are very low and there's not much to spend money on. In fact, there's darn little to spend our money on! Our bicycles have been the only major expense, and it will be no problem to sell them when we leave since there's a bicycle shortage here.

The weather here is "changeable." We must hear that remark 50 times a day! But it's true — we have about three days of warm weather and then three of cool weather; we've only had rain twice. The weather suits me fine, but all the students and "leaders" (administrators and teachers) are very concerned that we don't catch cold, that we don't overwork ourselves, that we enjoy the food, etc. Everything is fine; though, as you might guess, some things take getting used to.

Like spittoons. They're everywhere, and people use them constantly. And how long it takes to get anything official done. And I told you about the staring. And when we say "hello" in Chinese (which is about all we've mastered), they die of laughter. It's a very strange phenomenon. It's strange, too, having pictures of Marx, Lenin, Engels, Stalin, Mao and Hua Guofeng in our classrooms. Ian asked to be introduced to "those gentlemen" on the first day— which shocked and amused the students!

Our Chinese is minimal. But whenever we *do* have a problem, like finding our way, people are incredibly helpful and kind. Today, when Ian was trying to buy some beer, they didn't have any in the store, so they brought out a chair and made him sit in it while someone went off on a bike and got four bottles. From where, we don't know. And of course, everyone had a good look while he was sitting there.

We've been taken on a couple of excursions — to an old Buddhist temple, to a couple of parks, an ancient poet's home, and another excursion is planned for this weekend. This one is a set of sculptures designed to show "the cruelty of the landlords" before Liberation.

Well, I think I'd better push off to bed as it's getting late. Love to you both, and thanks for being such devoted letter writers.

DIARY ENTRY
Wednesday, May 21

We have been invited to a "dancing party" on Saturday at the Physics Department. (How progressive the Physics Department is! They also have the only washing machine on campus!) This is certainly a curious development and equally certainly a newly-revived custom. I don't know whether I dread it or am intrigued. We have been told only "15 pairs" can come (by which is meant 15 couples), as there is apparently not much room where it's held. We have been invited by a couple who teach English and the wife is the one who plied us with a million questions the night it was arranged for them to visit us: "Will you tape for us? Are you Christians? Are you members of the Communist Party? Didn't you bring your Bibles? What about materials for teaching intonation?" They have three sons, all of whom are attending university (a very high number for a Chinese family, especially one where both parents are intellectuals, not the preferred worker/ peasant/soldier background that, in the days of the Cultural Revolution, helped get one into university) and they are very bitter about the time that their sons "wasted" in the countryside as "sent-down" youth.

DIARY ENTRY
Thursday, May 22

After our Chinese lesson tonight, Li Xingui, our Chinese teacher, started translating Chinese poetry for us — Du Fu's poem, "Spring Rain": "Spring rain is as good as oil; it falls all over the ground." (It had started to rain during our lesson.) And one I liked better:

> Good rain knows exactly when to fall.
> It often falls in the spring,
> and it falls in the night,
> comes with the wind;

Here the translation broke down. Li's first love is Chinese literature but his knowledge of it isn't matched by his knowledge of English. The translation also broke down because Jiang, who was there too, was laughing his head off. Li said, "He's laughing because I am sensitive to poetry!" The next poem, called *Frost*, he was afraid would make us homesick for the snowy climes of Canada; I really liked his cryptic, broken translation:

> The moonlight into my window behind my bed.
> He wake and doubt if it is frost.
> He raise his head and saw the moon,
> and he lower his head and think of home.

"Oh, I know!" said Li, bothered, as we were, by Jiang's continued laughter. "It is not our duty to translate poems!"

· YOU'RE IN THE UNIT NOW ·

"You're in the unit now" was a song with forgettable verses that Ian and I improvised, adding sections to reflect new hurdles and burdens as we encountered them and accorded them a place in our daily or weekly routines. The creation of this song was a sort of sigh of resignation at the heaviness of the workload, an acceptance of the responsibilities and social location of the foreign expert role, and, I guess, a not entirely conscious realization that we had left behind an easier and less complex way of life for a stint in the *danwei*, the unit.

The work unit is central in the life of the Chinese city-dweller; it is usually both workplace and community. Once assigned to a work unit, an individual is assured a lifelong home and a salary — this is the concept of the "iron rice bowl," the guarantee of a livelihood (and the consequent freedom from hunger) that can never be broken, even if the individual's work performance is poor. Lately in China, there has been a debate about whether or not the "iron rice bowl" has outlived its usefulness or whether or not it seriously reduces production by fostering an indifferent work attitude. However, there have been no moves to dismantle this guarantee, which is such an impressive accomplishment in any country, especially in the Third World.

Besides promising work, a home and a salary for all its members, the unit is, to a certain degree, both self-sufficient and self-governing. It supports the families within it by providing necessities like health clinics, dining halls, child care and, sometimes, elementary schools. In addition, members may take advantage of the unit's sports and recreational activities, like basketball or movies. The unit also performs a political role: it can transmit its concerns to higher levels of authority — municipal, provincial or central Party — through the intermediary of the Party leadership. The leadership is, in turn, responsible for carrying out the policies of these authorities within the unit. The policies may be political in nature, like the study of directives from the Party or the implementation of new policies such as the One Child Movement; or they may be simply managerial, like the administration of the rationing system for grain, cooking oil and cotton.

In the cities of China, there are many types of units: productive units, organized around factory communities; work units for places like offices; administrative units; and in addition, living units for the downtown neighbourhoods or apartment complexes that form the core of Chinese cities. A youth finishing middle school (secondary school) registers with a central bureau of the city, which assigns individuals to their work units, generally on the basis of the need for workers registered by these different types of units. There seems to be an increasing attempt to match the individual's skills and interests with the kind of work unit he or she is assigned to. The assignment to a unit is, essentially, on a permanent basis, although transfers are possible. Within some cities, like Chengdu, the process of being placed in a unit takes about two or three months after graduation; in cities with high unemployment, like Shanghai, it may take as long as three or four years, reflecting the problem of a large pool of unemployed youth.

Unemployment in Shanghai is compounded by the presence of a large number of "social youth," a term which refers to the social problem these young people represent. These "social youth" have returned without permission from their assignments in the countryside as "sent-down youth." Living in Shanghai illegally, they are attached to no unit and therefore have no income. The "social youth" who have families in Shanghai must be supported by them; the means of support for those who have no family there is almost inconceivable.

Once assigned to a work unit, a young person would probably continue to live in his or her parents' unit until marriage. Living space considerations would be the main factor deciding whether a couple would settle in the husband's or wife's unit, assuming they are both working in the same city. When a young couple decides to get married, they inform the leadership of their units; the wedding date is set once they have a clear idea of when they can get a "room" in one of their units. This housing problem is one of the factors making divorce a very complicated event in China — one cannot simply move out and find a new apartment. The question of assigning a new unit, or a new room within the same unit, must be solved.

The main types of housing provided are either dormitories for single people and spouses living separately or one- or two-room apartments for nuclear families. It is extremely rare for a young Chinese person even to consider not getting married. The pattern of moving from the parental nuclear family to one's own nuclear family is astonishingly uniform. Therefore alternative lifestyles — for example, a group of unrelated adults or two people of the same sex living together — are almost an impossibility.

A major problem frequently pointed out by the Chinese is the fact that many spouses are forced to live in different cities because of the unit system, and may spend years seeing each other only at vacations. There were several such separations among our students and they occurred for various reasons. The critical accommodation shortage, a problem common to most cities in China, makes it very difficult for the units to absorb new members. Sometimes the leadership of a university is unwilling to lose a valuable faculty member by allowing him or her to transfer to a spouse's unit. And occasionally the bureaucratic complexities of arranging transfers prevent married couples from living together.

Living in the unit, I became aware of the extent to which the social organization of our lives in North America is fragmented. The spheres of family, friendship, school, work, the marketplace, public institutions and political community could, quite possibly, never intersect, and we must find our place in each of them. For the Chinese city-dweller, all these areas of his or her life are integrated within the unit. As difficult as it is for us to comprehend the "assigning" of a more or less permanent unit, the Chinese find the demands placed on us to make our way individually in each of these spheres both fascinating and terrifying. Our student teachers never stopped asking us about how our lives at home were organized, but they were amazed, for example, at the instability of jobs in the teaching profession in Canada. They found it puzzling and frightening that Ian and I could not count on having teaching careers for the rest of our lives.

Ian and I did not find it easy to become integrated into our unit, and I am not sure we ever discovered all the different activities going on within it. Sichuan University was a unit of 8000 people, including the families of the teachers, Party leaders and university workers, as well as the students. The number of students was said to have dropped to 2000 during the Cultural Revolution, but estimates for 1980 put the number between 3000 and 5000, closer to its pre-Cultural Revolution size of 5000.

The part of our unit with which we were the most familiar was the Foreign Language Department, but after we got our bearings we began to perceive a significant amount of work that was related more to the maintenance of the unit than to the education of the students. The unit operated a lumberyard, a carpentry shop and a sideline industry that produced pre-formed concrete, as well as employing a very large crew of workers who were constantly at work on new housing complexes. There was the mysterious nuclear plant, which I never found the time to visit. Each morning, on our way to class, we would pass many of the services provided in our unit: the barbershop, two small stores, the kindergarten, the movie theatre and the trade union building. On our way home from class, we would pass the bicycle repair shop as we headed for a stop we made every day — the post office, which also had a telephone. The university had, as well, many of the sports facilities we would expect on a campus: an outdoor swimming pool, a playing field, basketball courts. The unit owned three or four cars and several trucks, all of which were kept in excellent condition in the garage near the front gate of the unit (there are no private cars in China, except those of foreigners in Beijing; the cars and trucks are owned by the units and maintained by them). There was, of course, a clinic and perhaps a dozen "teaching buildings" for the different departments of the university. But the overwhelming impression, when we rode and walked around the unit, was of rows and rows of housing complexes.

Our little songwriting project was begun as we settled into a routine and started to gain a firm grasp of how to go about getting the things done that we wanted done. This was also the phase when we sensed the beginnings of mutual feelings of warmth and acceptance and attachment, feelings that were often evident in small incidents. One instance of this was the painstaking maps that one of the teachers in the department drew for us; these were maps of Chengdu, with the locations of various dumpling and specialty restaurants marked on them. He gave us these because he knew we'd enjoy being able to find these spots on our own, after he and his wife had once taken us to them. There was also the delight of the two-year old daughter of one of the women in the post office at our daily visits, and the tremendous encouragement that the kitchen staff gave us when they noticed our tiny improvements in Chinese. And with our students, it was the beginning of that easy period when it was possible for all of us to develop common jokes and routines and nicknames for each other.

We also, after our period of initial shock, began to learn how the Chinese customarily solve problems, and we took pleasure in adopting their solutions. For example, there was the delight at finding the widespread use of mosquito coils, a solution familiar from my own experience at cottages in Ontario ("Of course! These are imported from China!"), unlike our mosquito nets, which were a new experience. Our reliance on the omnipresent thermoses for hot water, our careful conserving of luxuries like plastic bags, our ability to find shops with bicycle pumps to fill our tires both in town and on the campus, our purchases of fruit in the "free markets" in town — all these were reassuring signs of adjustment and self-reliance.

It was also the period that I made the significant realization that there definitely were things I missed. My dormant coffee addiction reasserted its presence, for example. It had been shocked into quietude for the first month or so, and as I began to feel comfortable with my routine, I missed the familiar daily props of my life back home, and the old addictions began clamouring for their rightful place in my life. Consequently, these things began to be mentioned in my letters.

The *faux pas* we made in transgressing social conventions that are obvious to the Chinese were often great learning points for ourselves, our students and the other people we were close to. Taking our bicycles into our apartments at night, for example, was something we had to be told to do: no Chinese would leave his or her bike out for the night, for fear of its being stolen. We would feel very foolish if we forgot and brought ours in later than everyone else, or as occasionally happened, we left them out all night. What struck us about this custom was not so much the precaution that everyone faithfully took — there is, after all, in North America a great deal more bicycle theft, which we try to prevent with expensive locks and chains — but the fuss that would be made when we didn't follow the convention. These kinds of lapses gave our interpreters and students plenty of grief (What if a foreigner's bike were stolen?), and, gradually, we gained a sense of at least knowing *when* we were breaking rules.

During the difficult process of learning to cope with new situations, people often resort to feelings of superiority as an immediate, outraged defence against being considered inept. Ian and I frequently gave the people around us in the unit plenty of evidence that we had to be resocialized, like children. We would sometimes find ourselves defensively presenting the idea that, within our own culture, we *were* adequately socialized. For someone in my profession, teaching immigrants English back home in Canada, it was an extremely valuable lesson to learn to meet these points of conflict without a sense of judgement, and I can't say that I have accomplished this to my own satisfaction. Some of my letters show that, despite an openness and curiosity about new customs, I had not yet internalized this lesson.

Friday, May 23, 1980
Dear Robin and Michael and kids,

I found out something today that I thought might interest you, and that's a senior professor's teaching load: two to four hours a week of lecturing. Now, that's reasonable, but what knocked my socks off was that this occurs usually only one year out of three! (Rarely, two years out of three.) The other two years are devoted to research. Very junior people teach six to 12 hours a week yearly.

It's been pretty difficult getting information on how the university is structured and we have to put together bits and pieces, and we usually come up against a brick wall: the Cultural Revolution, which is the source of all disruption, inefficiency and lack of teaching expertise. One thing that surprised me was the size of the university faculties: in the Physics Department, for example, there are 100 teachers and 200 students. Not all of the people not teaching are senior ones doing research, but plenty are junior ones taken on during the Cultural Revolution who are not very well-qualified, but who are doing some restraining. And that's the case with most of our students — they're college teachers whose English needs upgrading.

I don't know where we fit on the teaching scale, but our workload is lots heavier — 16 hours of teaching, plus lectures once weekly to the whole department, "tutorial hours" two afternoons a week. The other afternoons we're kept busy taping scripts and scripting tapes for the language lab. Then there are excursions in the evenings and on Sundays with our students — not to mention preparation and correction. There seems to be some misapprehension that since we're native speakers of English, we don't need to prepare!

It seems incredible that we've been here a month. We've slipped into a routine, of sorts, but there's been plenty that hasn't been easy to get used to: constant use of spittoons, the language, demented bicycle traffic, constant honking of horns on cars — and what's been most staggering is the lack of basic knowledge of the West. Things that have been easy to get used to have been the splendid food, the wonderful Chinese beer, and the (so far) very mild weather.

Well, there's tons I haven't mentioned — this experience is just so enormously different that it's hard to know where to begin. And it will so soon be over.

DIARY ENTRY
Saturday, May 24

Adventures and accomplishments! We rode into town with Michael's words that we were "brave" to be attempting what we were planning ringing in our ears. We managed the following with no help:

- to place transoceanic calls to our families via the office at the Jin Jiang Hotel (no English speakers among the staff at the hotel);
- to locate the post office near the Worker Peasant Soldier Department Store (I'm very fond of that store's name!);
- to mail the roll of film (labelled "used film" in English and Chinese) and the tape we made (labelled "used cassette tape");
- to locate the Friendship Store (the first time without being taken there);

- to find the Café Vienna and get some pastries "to go";
- to buy a smelly yellow oilcloth umbrella each, which will horrify Miss Li because she is certain we like modern synthetic things and she has been trying to put us off getting these;
- to return to the dining hall by noon for lunch.

When we arrived at lunch, I asked Michael if we looked like cats that had eaten canaries. Smug city.

This evening, there was an annoying merry-go-round of weird developments, that I am unlikely ever to get to the bottom of. At 29 minutes past 7, one minute before we were to be picked up for the "dancing party," Jiang and the son of the couple who invited us arrived to tell us it was cancelled. It was mysterious that the party had been called off, because we'd been told that the Physics Department has these dances regularly, every week. The fact that we'd been invited to this one seemed to have something to do with its being cancelled. The son demanded assurances from Jiang that another dancing party would be held; I guess he was upset because he's in the Physics Department and must have been organizing this party especially for us. Perhaps because Jiang is a Party member, he was in on the decision to cancel it. I carefully explained the whole incident to Michael, and he was as puzzled as we were. Also disappointed. He was looking forward to a description of the event, because up till recently dancing hasn't really been permitted.

Essentially, Ian and I were relieved because we are both still sick, and could really use the rest; we were also not relishing the spectacle of being put on display as dancing partners, oog. But we did feel a little piqued at these last-minute changes and the fact that none of this was in our hands. And I'm also sure that although we might have been pretty uncomfortable, we missed an interesting experience.

I had put on a pretty blouse for the event. Was it Emma Goldman who said, "If I can't dance, I don't want to be part of your revolution"? She wouldn't approve of this mysterious cancellation.

Try as I might, however, I cannot convince anyone that dancing is *not* one of my favourite recreations; everyone just *knows* this is how Westerners enjoy themselves.

"Oh, Ian," I said, "I feel so self-conscious when everyone is watching me dance."

"Oh, *I* don't," he replied, founding a routine that has now become a custom with us — negating obvious statements. We figure the stating of the obvious ("We're going over a bridge now") is a standard part of Chinese small talk.

Sunday, May 25
Dear Robert,

By now you're probably beginning to have that all-too-familiar feeling about Toronto — if you operate at all the way I do it takes about three days before I start feeling that I've never been away. So, how was it? Did you get to see much of Ireland? And what about the Continent? Ah, Paris!

This is crazy, to be in the middle of China, thinking about Paris. But Paris has some things we really miss (as do most cities) and I guess the main thing is being able to go and sit in a café and drink *coffee!* and not move for two hours.

There are lots of reasons why we can't do that here, and the lack of coffee is not the chief one. The other problem is that we can't go anywhere, or stop anywhere, without a crowd of people gathering around us to stare at us. Children point and giggle, whole busloads of people crane their necks out of windows as we pass, bicycle traffic is endangered, and honest to God, we cause traffic jams, because people get off their bikes and stop dead in the street, which gathers more people and then the trucks can't get through.

We feign nonchalance about riding our bikes to the interpreters because they're worried about us having an accident, but in reality, riding a bike in the city is mighty dangerous.

Our students are overwhelmingly friendly and almost devoted. They see this course as the chance of a lifetime, second only to being able to study abroad, and work their fingers to the bone, to use a cliché. Clichés are on my mind because that's how our students speak and write — in formulas, the extravagant prose you find in Maoist literature ("Tempered in struggle, like a bamboo shoot after a spring rain, the people's consciousness is maturing steadily . . ."). We've been working hard with them to get them to speak and write more naturally, but there's an enormous cultural conflict behind all this.

We have some special favourite people among the comrades who deal with us. One is comrade Li, who's teaching us Chinese two evenings a week. I'd like to ship him home with my bike (actually, he probably wouldn't mind!). Learning Chinese is just about the most difficult thing I've ever attempted. I can barely keep my numbers straight, and that's usually the first thing I learn in a foreign country. Being a language teacher and feeling like the most stunned student I've ever had is, I suppose, an excellent experience.

This is an interesting time to be here, politically. Critical noises are being made about Mao and there is universal condemnation of the Cultural Revolution. Many of the leaders "persecuted" during the CR are now having their names restored, and in the case of Liu Shao-qi, it's been done posthumously. Things is *really* changin!

It's a cloudy grey Sunday morning and since the gas is on all day Sunday, I've been boiling a pot of water so that I can have a one-inch hot bath. Think of me the next time you take a bath (showers are a thing of the past).

Your little alarm clock forms part of the intricate system of noises that is designed to wake me up. Chinese music for exercises and indecipherable chatter comes blaring over the loudspeakers at 6 a.m., and continues till 8; my Westclox rings at 6:30 and the little digital beeps at 6:45; and at 7:15 Ian pounds at my door to pick me up for breakfast. Just this week, I've started to get over my incredible exhaustion. (This, I think is the form my culture shock took — trying to understand everything wears me out; and it was compounded by having to do all my preparation between 11 and 2 a.m., after the guests leave.) Now I'm no longer sleeping through the first three noises. Classes start at 8! Some final thoughts: the beer is excellent, though it's never cold. Cigarettes are very strong. There's plenty of pollution. And why don't you tear off a note or two — even postcards are a major treat.

DIARY ENTRY
May 25

Spent a wonderfully peaceful Sunday morning writing letters, and then out in the sunshine of the front courtyard washing the mud-caked bike, which has been drawing great disapproval from our students. Here is an area where I find my values completely the reverse of the Chinese: everyone keeps their bikes spic and span, and tucks little oily rags of "waste cotton" under the seats. These are used for cleaning as soon as a speck of dirt appears. I'm sure, consequently, that many of the bikes that we think are new are simply very well taken care of. I prefer to ride my bike until the wheels won't turn from dried mud being packed in the works, while I consider keeping my terrazzo floors spotless an absolute necessity. The way Ian and I try to keep our floors clean seems an inexplicably neurotic obsession to the people who know about it. One of my chief frustrations is the ineffective mop that I have to drag around the floors — a bamboo pole with one-inch wide strips of cotton cloth tied to it. I have to admit, though, that it's easier by far to keep a bike clean.

After dinner tonight, we decided to throw caution to the winds, and took a number 3 bus for four stops to the hotel. I had a moment of terror as the bus sped out into the countryside; this, after a moment of exultation at my competence — I'd inquired of the woman ticket-taker if the bus we were getting on was "san" (number 3) and she'd replied "Sanwa!", and I figured that was close enough. I couldn't imagine what we'd do if we had gotten on the wrong bus. Anyway, the bus soon careened back into familiar territory. I told Ian that I hadn't been so frightened since I was in Hong Kong, going to the train station to get on the train to God-Knew-What in China.

We watched the news in one of the TV rooms in the hotel, and then parked ourselves in the bar while some highly emotive drama unfolded on the TV there and the tourists (envy!) relaxed. We ordered Tsingtao beer, bought chocolate (Ian had peanuts) and proceeded to sigh over the ordeal of creating something "fun" for the students for the next day's classes. We prepared our joint panel, I planned my lecture and got all my correcting done. Michael arrived later and joined us. I admitted to them both that my spirits had been slumping, but that I felt like a new woman after such a relaxing, productive evening.

Of course, we hadn't completely thrown caution to the winds, because we still haven't worked our courage up to the state where we can ride our bikes back to the university in the pitch black. I can understand why people don't have lights and reflectors on their bikes (money) but it's beyond me why drivers don't use their lights in the total darkness.

Tuesday, May 27
Dear Penny,

A short dash of a note. We're thinking of you as your birthday approaches, and eagerly looking in the mail for reports on all events.

Teaching continues. A heavy load. This whole experience is a 24-hour-a-day thing, and we are getting expert at sneaking off (tsk!) in our quote free time unquote — which is when the entire teaching and student body chooses to "drop in" and have "free conversation." Oh, my nerves, as my mother would say. I had a minor crisis over the unsuitability of our teaching techniques, but it was a private one, and nobody, not even the students, noticed. It's rough going, figuring out what they need (everything) and how to give it to them.

It's a beautiful, sunny, mild day today. Just the day for a bike ride...Ah, the simple pleasures of life. Ian and I are, by the way, living proof of the "critical period" hypothesis of language learning [which proposes that there is a biologically determined age beyond which the learning of a second language becomes increasingly difficult].

May 27
Dear Mary Ellen,

How are your plans to get up here in July? There are some mutterings, but very vague, about our having a few days in July to go to a local site, Mt. E Mei, but given the level of, well, everything, we'll probably be the last to know what exactly's going on.

Anyway, it would be, let me reiterate, absolutely wonderful to have you here.

It's taken us *so* long to get any kind of familiar sense about Chengdu. I still feel wary bicycling into town —

fear of getting lost — because we've been under such close guard for so long. But slowly and surely, we are making a determined march in our trek to conquer the unknown territories...

What do you do about prose like that, by the way?

I'm experiencing so many conflicts about the teaching. On the one hand, the war against perpetual explication of text is a "just battle," on the other, I'm getting worn out, and have begun to wonder whether it's worth it. I can understand and sympathize with what our students perceive as their needs — to be able to confidently and competently answer *their* students' grammatical/textual questions, in a system where they have very little control over content and methodology.

And, oh, we have so much work to do. Which is another reason why I'm weary. Ah, well, you know all this.

About *our* problems: as I said in my other letter, the spirit duplicating fluid and the paper is the stuff we need; if you could get it at the place you checked out in Hong Kong and put it on the train to us, we'd be forever grateful...and so would our students. There's not much else we really need, though tons of things we want (like coffee and treats, and stuff like Ajax to clean our bathtubs, but really, they're all inessentials).

Now that I'm here, I feel like a heel not having asked if there was anything we could have brought you from Canada. We were so loaded down and befuddled that we didn't understand what a nice treat it would have been.

Anyway, we really, really hope your plans to get here are materializing. We'd love some company! And besides, think of the irresistible Sichuan food...

DIARY ENTRY
Wednesday, May 28

Last week, when the city was invaded by a horde of white butterflies, little boys were everywhere, maliciously whipping at them with sticks, seemingly just to pass the time. We did see one family whose father was catching them in a butterfly net. But one little boy was doggedly stalking a butterfly with a *brick*, trying to drop it on the poor critter. Gave new meaning to the expression, "killing a fly with a hammer."

Have had a really excellent couple of mornings teaching, which have followed quite hearteningly on the heels of a disastrous slide show on Canada I gave the department. An agonizing silence followed, a silence I didn't have the authority to end — I suggested that if there were no more questions, we could adjourn, but no one made a move because the head of the department hadn't assented. So I stood at the front, frantically concocting questions for myself to answer. My students later explained that they hadn't asked any questions because they didn't know anything about the subject.

It is no exaggeration to say that this is the most difficult teaching I've ever done because it is so hard to figure out needs; and what we think these people need is different from what they think (but do not say) they need. And what *we* desperately need is our duplicating machine.

Thursday, May 29
Dear Michael and Kevin,

I just got a letter from your Nan and she wrote that you had your mother busy washing clothes on Mother's Day, all for the sake of soccer. Soccer's a pretty popular game here, but volleyball and basketball are even more popular. Kids, especially little boys in grade school, are *really* good at ping-pong. But by the time they get to high

school, they think ping-pong is kid's stuff and are more
interested in track and field or volleyball. Or swimming.

Everyone rides a bike. There are *lots* more bicycles
than cars or trucks. The roads are filled with them, and
everyone rides wherever they're going without really
looking. You would be shocked. But there is a loud bell
on each bike, and people use them a lot — so that when
you're riding around in the city, especially after you've
been to a movie where a big crowd is getting out, the air
is filled with the tinkling of bicycle bells! And even
though there aren't very many cars, the drivers constantly
honk their horns. Even here at the university, which is
far from downtown, you can hear lots of horns and bells
in the background. We're really glad to have our bikes
because we can get out into the countryside (and see rice
paddies and wheat fields, with lots of people working in
them) or into the city with the crazy traffic.

I have a new name. It's Han Lin — here your last name
comes first, and "Han" is the closest thing to "Hynes." I
like it.

Every morning at 6 o'clock, the people living at the
university are woken up by music and talking on the
loudspeakers. Most people go out and do some exercises,
especially Tai Chi Chuan, which is like karate, only
slower and more beautiful to watch. An old Daoist monk
invented this martial art a long time ago after watching a
fight between a heron and a snake. Mostly older people
do Tai Chi here. And at the end of the working day,
between 5 and 6, people do more exercises. Most people
get a lot of exercise and are very strong from all the hard
work they do, even the children. In the evening, after
supper, the families sit around in the courtyard and relax — the kids play hide-and-seek, or practise riding on
the big bike in the family (most families have only one
bike).

Well, Michael and Kevin, I'd like to remind a certain
pair of brothers that they still haven't written to tell me
who's winning the Stanley Cup, or any other Canadian

news. We really miss everyone, and getting a letter is a big treat. All my students save Canadian stamps, too.

DIARY ENTRY
Thursday, May 29

The essential failure of the Chinese Revolution is that it has never eradicated allergies. I've also discovered some evidence for the importance of teaching language in a meaningful context: one of the first verbs Ian and I learned in Chinese and one I'm sure we'll retain all our lives, is "to wheeze." And one sentence I've never taught before to beginning English classes: "The distinguished foreign guest is wheezing." I, an experienced wheezer, am not surprised by my body's reaction to the heavy pollution, but Ian has never wheezed in his life, and is a little nonplussed by it. "Oh, you have newcomer's cough," said a former Canadian Embassy official when we ran into him in the Friendship Store. "Newcomer's cough, you mean there's a syndrome?" we asked, astonished, and just a little rueful that we hadn't known to expect this. "Well, I thought people got it only in Beijing."

We spent the evening teaching Zhu, the leader who has direct control over us, how to play Scrabble. It was the first pleasant, relaxing evening we'd spent with him. We got him to show us on the Chinese map that we put up on the wall where he's from, and he admitted to us that he is quite often homesick. When I asked him if he went home on vacations, he said he couldn't afford the train ride every year — so that he usually goes every other year.

DIARY ENTRY
Friday, May 30

For the last period of the day on Mondays and Fridays, Ian and I hold what we call "panels": we bring the two classes together in a big classroom on the first floor of the Foreign Language Building, and the two of us sit at a large desk at the front of the room with a bank of tape recorders in front of us. One of us then "interviews" the other on some predetermined topic. Topics we have done are work in North America, leisure, our educational system, the holidays we celebrate, the family; we have requests to do some on religion, unions, the overseas Chinese and unemployment. Soon we'll be using this time to show the slides that Mary Ellen lent us; they're organized into different facets of life of Westerners in big cities — things like shopping, entertainment, education, transportation, work, politics. This is also the time that we show films, when we have them.

Today's topic was a concession to the pressure on Maureen as Foreign Charlatan to lecture on Western Philosophy, since that's what her undergraduate degree is in, and on Ian to teach French as well as English, since that's what *his* MA is in.

We chose to do a panel on the life of Jean-Paul Sartre, since he just died in April. We talked about his importance in philosophy, literature and in politics, and introduced these teachers to the term "existentialism." I was interested in their reactions to what I had prepared on Sartre's personal life, his relationship with Simone de Beauvoir, and her feminist work. I explained that Sartre and de Beauvoir had never married because they believed that marriage is a bourgeois institution that supports property relations in a capitalist society. The students reacted with rich, hearty chuckles to this puzzling notion. And why not? Here is a society that has pretty well managed to get rid of property relations without dismantling the institution of marriage.

DIARY ENTRY
Saturday, May 31

Children's Day was celebrated today. Many groups of little pioneers — red scarves around their necks, three dots of lipstick on their faces, one on each cheek, and one, oddly, on their foreheads — were marched around the city by adults. After today, apparently, we can wear skirts. Xiao Ho suggested I stop wearing "that blue jean" and said that if I wore a skirt, "we will follow your lead." I asked, "Is there a special date when you can start wearing skirts?" "Yes," said Ho, "Children's Day, June 1." "And what about short sleeves?" "You may have the possibility of wearing that after May Day."

An attack of diarrhea, cramps, coughing and exhaustion put me back to bed after breakfast, until 11 or so, when Jiang woke me up by knocking at the door. Tousled, in my nightgown, groggy, I was greeted with the question, "Were you reading books?"

Later in the afternoon, I decided I could handle a bike ride into town. On our way into the post office, we were overtaken by a very gabby, insistent young student wanting to shepherd us around all day, and who would not, despite repeated requests, take the hint that we wanted to be on our own.

These young students are so frantically anxious for a chance to practise their English and have "free conversation" that they will latch onto any *waiguo ren*, and not leave you in peace until you throw a tantrum. I don't mind people wanting to chat for a bit, or riding along with us, but these people take charge and assume the interpreter role that we so desperately want to escape. Michael understood; he suggested we speak French to such people.

Anyway, we parked our bikes outside the Worker Peasant Soldier Department Store, in the "parking lot" that is run by a different old woman each time we go, paid our one *fen* fee to have her guard them (getting in return a little bamboo marker that has to be surrendered

to pick up the bike), and walked into the store to browse.
Ah, to browse, which would have been impossible with
Miss Li or the student who overtook us; I think they find
the crowds that gather around us every time we pause as
disconcerting as we do, but will not admit it to us, and so
handle it by never allowing us to pause. We bought all
kinds of essentials: a flashlight, a nailbrush, some toilet
paper, tea, glue, a notebook, and of all things, a rubber
acupuncture doll. Such pleasure. And to think it had all
been threatened by the student who latched onto us. To
dodge our interpreters only to have a stranger pull the
same trick!

韩琳

Sunday, June 1
Dear Mary Ellen,

Thanks for the letter — great news! I've brought the
matter of your visit up again, and it is fine for you to stay
here and eat here as well. So! All set! Also have found
out that our trip to Mt. E Mei will probably be in August
or September, so there's no conflict there. Of course, with
the law of irony that rules my life, your letter arrived the
day after I sent you one.

A strange thing happened today. We got a letter (on
Sunday?) that was delivered by Ian's interpreter, Jiang. It
was addressed to "Foreign Experts, F.L. Department,
Sichuan University," and it was already opened. Jiang
said matter-of-factly as he handed it to us, "I read that
letter." Someday soon, we'll have to inform him, and a
few others, that that is a gigantic no-no in the eyes of
foreigners. Lowering the cultural boom.

Anyway, the letter was from two American experts at
Jilin University in Changchun, and they were writing to
find out about our Ministry of Education Teacher
Training program (do we give methodology classes?

practice teaching? know any useful texts?). They thought some "articulation" between the experts would be useful and have been trying to set up (or I guess explore the possibility of setting up) a conference of foreign experts doing teacher training. The higher-ups have not been biting, as you might guess. I especially liked one line in her letter: "Ah, the elusive leaders..."

Thought you might be interested in that bit of gossip on the expert circuit, especially because of the conference you were trying to set up last year.

And about what you could get us in Hong Kong, besides the spirit duplicator fluid and the paper — ah, a deep sigh. First of all, we'll need some of that correcting fluid for the stencils. You know the kind? Not the typewriter white-out stuff, but the stuff that's like nail polish (and if you can't get any, a bottle of nail polish or two will do in a pinch!). This sounds crazy, but if you see an egg-timer, grab it. The one with my Perquacky game broke in transit. Our students at first scorned such activity but now we can't tear them away from Scrabble. I could use some baby powder or talcum powder or dusting powder (the less scented, the better). Ian wouldn't mind some Head and Shoulders shampoo and two sticks of "nice" deodorant (not spray, not roll on). And the Ajax.

The above are not crucial necessities, just pleasant additions (except the nail polish!). As we descend to the level of outright inessential luxuries, we find things like some good coffee, some liquor and treats like that. Oh, I forgot: two toasted bacon and tomato sandwiches, with mayonnaise (brown bread, please) (bacon crisp) (no lettuce on mine).

Well, what did you think of the referendum results? We interrupted our Chinese lesson to pull in VOA that night and got the 60% *non* and 40% *oui* results. Ian had been expecting a *oui*, since he'd been working in a CÉGEP all year in Montreal and thought the 18-year-olds' votes would swing it. Oh, well, now I guess Pierre can retire and travel, just as he's always wanted. "There are rooms for discussion," as one of my students here wrote in a composition.

One last purchase request: some strong cough medicine (stuff like Benylin with codeine) and strong cough drops. The pollution and pollen and dust and culture shock have been expressing themselves through our respiratory systems (or perhaps it's because we haven't been using the spittoons). I got some Chinese cough medicine which is pretty good (plus delicious) but I don't want to be going back to the clinic a lot for it because it just gives our interpreters one more chance to be busybodies about our lives. ("Maureen, you're coughing. Put on more clothes. Take your medicine. You better see the doctor. Have a good rest.") Of course we will reimburse you for all this.

Well, I'm gonna go because all I will do if I continue is think of more things for you to buy. Looking forward to the great event!

DIARY ENTRY
June 1

I was wrong about Children's Day being celebrated yesterday; they were just practising. It was today. We went to the Chuke Liang Temple Park with six of our nicest students, and I think every child in Chengdu was in that park, staring at us. The crowds gathering around us were just shorter than usual, that's all. It was extraordinary — a knot of kids would spot us, whoop with delight, and race over to us pell-mell, gathering others as they gained momentum. Ian was of course in his element and delighted the kids with his silliness. It was a splendid, calm, friendly outing, and we had to troop all over unknown parts of Chengdu to get there, so we had lots of time to chat with the students.

韓琳

Monday, June 2
Dear Mom and Dad,

We're sitting on Ian's balcony, a nice breeze blowing after a warm sunny day — evening, all the kids playing in the courtyard and families strolling around. The weather has been quite hot on a couple of days, but cools off again very quickly. There is a very rigid attitude to dress here: it's like when we were kids and you, Mom, would try and make us wear boots until the 24th of May (but it never worked). Men don't wear short sleeves until May Day (May 1) and women don't start wearing skirts (they're much cooler) until Children's Day, June 1. Oh, yes, Mom, remember telling me whenever I asked why there was no Children's Day, "*Every* day is Children's Day"? — well, in China, there's a Children's Day.

It was celebrated yesterday — Sunday — and we went to a temple and park — and I think every child in Chengdu was there and followed us around.

You asked about radio broadcasts in English. With much frustrated fiddling on the shortwave, we can pull in the BBC and the Voice of America. Plenty of interference and crackling. Sometimes, when we're feeling energetic, we jump on our bikes and ride to the hotel downtown and watch the Chinese news on colour TV (there aren't too many TVs here, but the ones there are in public places are all colour). When they have the international news, it's via satellite, and the Chinese broadcasters speak over the English — but we can still pick up a bit. So we saw CBS-type news on the Mt. Helen eruption.

韓琳

Monday, June 2
Dear David and Ian,

David, thanks a million for the *Maclean's* — we (and our students!) fell on it and devoured even the most inane articles. The issue you sent had a picture of a man wearing a three-piece suit: this was something that had just come up in a reading and I was able to display the ad showing the very thing. Not to mention the photos of Jean-Paul Sartre and Simone de Beauvoir, whom we'd just done a panel and listening piece on. Very handy in all.

David, it didn't take long to figure out what, at first reading, puzzled me in the note that you gave me to read on the airplane, about "loving and hating China" with equal enthusiasm. I'm constantly irked by the extraordinary caution the interpreters and "leaders" exercise over all our doings. Sometimes we just need to hop on our bikes and ride into town or into the countryside, to get away from being guided through our lives. Although it's plenty difficult to negotiate our pleasures and business without this help, it's also a great joy to be able to taste the freedom.

The teaching is going well, I think. I am still cracking my brains over how to simultaneously teach a linguistic competence-type course along with a teacher-training course and it's quite a challenge. I'm not satisfied with how much we've been able to get done, but I suppose some time is always lost at the beginning just figuring out needs and suitable methods.

A political observation: I'm surprised at the extent of the criticism of Mao. There was a memorial service on May 17 for Liu Shaoqi, the biggest "capitalist roader" of them all during the Cultural Revolution. He was exonerated and the opportunity taken (in building this event) to point out that Mao was quite responsible for the ill treatment of Liu (not misled by Jiang Qing and the rest of the Gang of Four, as has been the previous point of view). We have our students keep diaries, which we mark once a week, and they're an excellent source of opinion both on what we're doing in the classes, and on what's going on politically. Some students remarked that Mao, unlike certain present leaders, had not been abroad to study "foreign democracies" but had made a study of Chinese feudalism in order to mix his "second-hand Marxism" with his attempt to be a "life-long emperor." Awfully harsh words, in my opinion. An indication of things to come? Besides the universal condemnation of the Cultural Revolution, people express more tentatively a certain embarrassment over the former sway of "Mao Zedong Thought." I dunno. These are extremely interesting times to be here, but all the developments make me pretty nervous. The vice-premier visiting the U.S. to purchase military equipment?

Well, a certain distinguished foreign guest is nodding off and getting writer's cramp at the same time. Thanks again for all the help and support the month before we left. Oh, and Ian — you were absolutely right about Ian Gertsbain: there couldn't be a better person for going around, kicking pedestals out from under people as they "stand on ceremony" (while telling us not to). We've had quite a lot of good times with people laughing and singing and joking — times when, at the beginning of the evening, everyone has been so prim that fun looked out of the question. Ian just won't allow people to remain formal for long. Plus we have many private guffaws as well.

Hope you're both starting a fine summer.

韓琳

DIARY ENTRY
Tuesday, June 3

Miss Li runs into a beautiful young woman, a former fellow student who graduated in the class ahead of her. We're in the Jin Jiang Hotel, outside *Luxingshe*, the China Travel Service office; they have a brief conversation and part. Miss Li turns to me and says, "She's a travel guide." "Oh," I reply, "that's a nice job. She's lucky." "Do you think so?" Miss Li asks with genuine surprise. "Sure," I say, "you get to travel, meet foreigners, and all that. I wouldn't mind that job at all." "I think it's more honourable to be a teacher," responds Miss Li. And then it is my turn to be surprised. I didn't understand that such concepts as "honour" were still so extant, though I knew that the teacher or scholar or intellectual was traditionally very prestigious.

We're getting a little worried about what arrangements are being made for our beds unbeknownst to us. In the courtyard today, lots of straw mats were hung out to dry or air, I don't know which. Once, in one of the stores that Miss Li took us into — one of the shopping expeditions that is all a blur because we were so sick — we took an interest in the mats. Nice rugs, we'd thought they'd be. No, no, all wrong, they were for beds and pillows in the hot weather. Last week Miss Li said we'd be getting them to replace the thin padded mats we have because they're cooler to sleep on. We're a little alarmed because we don't quite know how this custom works, but if it means taking away the padded mats and putting these sheets of straw matting down on the bare springs, which are barely softened by the padding, we're going to find comfortable sleeping impossible.

韓琳

103

DIARY ENTRY
Thursday, June 5

I have finally learned what upset Jiang and Miss Li so much about my choice in bikes. I thought my bike looked very standard, exactly like 95 per cent of all the other bikes in Chengdu—black, 28 inches, a man's, no gears of course, the caliper lock on the back wheel. I chose it over a dinky 24-inch woman's model like Miss Li's because it reminded me of my own Raleigh (on which, I hear, Chinese bikes are modelled).

But this week, as I was getting on my bike outside the Foreign Language building, a student in the department came up and started chatting. His eyes kept straying to my bicycle. Finally he touched it and said, "Why did you buy a peasant's bicycle?"

"A peasant's bicycle?" I asked. "What do you mean?"

He showed me the two extra steel rods that run between the hub of the front wheel and the centre of the handlebars. Of course I had noticed them, but I didn't know what they were for. "These are to make the bike stronger, for carrying heavy loads," he explained.

I realized then, something Jiang and Miss Li would never have told me: I was essentially choosing a bike much below my status. Not just a woman, not just an intellectual, but a foreigner—riding a peasant's bicycle!

Slowly, slowly, I am beginning to be able to discern the Jaguars from the Honda Civics.

Friday, June 6
Dear Diane and Ben and Tessa baby,

Ian and I are sitting on his balcony in the spare 30 minutes we have today — just after dinner, just before our Chinese lesson. It's very hot, but we are treating ourselves to a cup of our execrable Chinese instant coffee, having had a big bottle of Chinese beer with a wonderful Chinese dinner of dumplings. There are a zillion kids in the courtyard below and they are all heartmeltingly cute. Some have hairstyles like (a) but most have (b). Very tiny ones have (c) and older girls have (d). A variation on (b), suitable for all ages, is (e). As for the pretty baby clothes, I dunno. None of the clothes for kids I've seen in stores (or on kids) looks specially Chinese — just T-shirts and pants and very ordinary dresses or skirts. Not the kind of thing that, if you put them on Tessa, passersby would stop and demand to know where you'd gotten the cute Chinese outfit.

(a)   (b)   (c)   (d)   (e)

I've already told Miss Li about your request for baby clothes, which puzzled her no end. But she did promise me a trip to the Children's Department Store in Chengdu. The department stores are, like everything here, very hard to describe — like one-floor general stores — dusty, dark, old, very crowded. One of my favourites, the Worker Peasant Soldier Department Store is a rambling, ramshackle affair — you can turn a corner and find yourself in a section of it that is actually an outdoor alley lined with counters.

It's hard to imagine, unless you've been in a place like Cuba, the unavailability of things and the limited selection of goods. But it's unavailability in a different way — I remember walking through department stores in Cuba that had three or four items on each shelf. Here, the stores are crammed with goods, and the counters are full. It's just that in a country of a billion people, with the mass of people shopping daily, it's striking how quickly things run out and are not replaced. So one law of shopping I have had to acquire (that Ian has always had) is that if you see something you need/want — buy it. It won't be there the next day (unless it's expensive).

Cotton, and therefore cotton clothing, is rationed — you have to have coupons to get it. This, however, doesn't apply to distinguished foreign guests. We pay higher prices for cotton and the other rationed commodity we use — grain. Two sets of prices.

We don't cook for ourselves, so we don't need to buy rice or flour, but when people get rice in the restaurants, or cakes and cookies in stores, they hand over their grain coupons as they pay. We aren't, as I said, issued ration coupons, and we are simply charged a higher price for rationed items. A fair enough system considering our salaries are four or five times that of most people.

And the other thing is that all the babies wear slit pants, no diapers. So babies and toddlers just squat down anywhere and poop or pee. Not only do diapers, excuse me, nappies, not exist; but neither do tampax or sanitary pads (women simply use toilet paper.)

Many people had warned me that our status as distinguished foreign experts is higher than most experts' (having been chosen for this cultural exchange by the Canadian government rather than being directly employed by the Chinese, as most experts are), so I had prepared myself for the "red carpet treatment." Well, we have been put to work and given so little free time that we can barely keep our eyes open when we are taken on an outing.

Our students accompany us on these outings — one "evening joking party" that is, a comedy show and a ballet; also three visits to parks in the city — and use the opportunity to have "free conversation." This is fine when we've got a nice bunch with us, but sometimes students prepare and memorize a speech about the park, and recite it to us as we walk along, "This park is both fascinating and fanciful, I think..."

I wonder what it would be like for you to come here and do my job. Our students would be fascinated by a living example of an Overseas Chinese. I've never heard of a *Chinese* foreign expert, and that would be an interesting prospect...

DIARY ENTRY
Early Saturday morning, June 7

I am not a squeamish female. I really don't mind bats or even snakes, as long as they're not indoors. I thought it was kind of friendly that Hector the chicken or that frog wanted to come into my apartment. I didn't mind the rat I pointed out to Ian, the one that was poking its head out of the hole in the wall opposite the garage.

In this apartment there are enormous moths, June bugs, spiders, even a grasshopper with one leg that took three days to die in my bathroom after I refused to touch it, not to mention the run-of-the-mill ants, cockroaches, caterpillars, mosquitoes and teeny harmless flying bugs that gather near the lights at night.

But the lizard on the wall above my window in the living room has freaked me out. I've locked my bedroom door and closeted myself in here, scared that it will scrabble in through one of the cracks and crawl all over me in my sleep. I *like* lizards. But not in my house.

DIARY ENTRY
Saturday, June 7

Ian remarked today that *none* of the staring that gets us down is sexual, a fact that had really escaped my conscious notice till now. Then I remembered my travels in Europe, and the constant hassles and sexual advances that I encountered. The kind of attention we get here, though ennervating, really is preferable: people simply are curious, and in a funny way, really are "filled with admiration," as the students and interpreters put it.

Accomplished today on our own: bicycle seat fixed at the repair shop on campus, telegram to Embassy sent, birthday telegram to Penny sent, one bath taken, a good long nap taken, a small lunch negotiated in the hotel, a message in Chinese cancelling lunch tomorrow communicated to the kitchen staff, two maps of the world purchased. My personal accomplishment: one Scrabble game lost.

DIARY ENTRY
Sunday, June 8

Today we had the visit to the Rent-Collector's Courtyard; in all, a splendid visit and well worth the jagged, harrowing, blasting bus ride through the "periodic market day" of a couple of villages. Some images I wasn't quick enough to catch on film: two baskets of baby chicks, hanging from a shoulder-pole a man was carrying; a truckload of hairy, black-snouted pigs milling around under our noses as the truck crawled by our bus; an "aged man" thrown onto a tree trunk hanging precariously over a ditch, the result of his swerving to avoid our bus — when everybody realized he was unharmed, they laughed merrily. And so on through the rice paddies, shuddering at the narrow misses and the incessant horn honking.

"You know what they're doing?" asked Wen Bau, pointing to a group of women working in the paddies with very long bamboo poles. "Hoeing?" "No — weeding." Strangely enough, a different student asked me the same question in the same words on the way back, and looked very pleased when I knew the answer.

A young peasant woman carrying one of those poles sticking well out into the middle of the road made the bus driver swerve to a stop and blat horrendously on the horn. If he hadn't stopped, the pole would have splintered the windshield.

This visit to the countryside brought the population of China into real focus for me; usually we think of the countryside as an area less populated than the city, but in all the "county seats" (towns) we passed through, there was such a tremendous crush of people gathering for the free markets that the bus could scarcely make its way through the main streets.

And so we got "Class Education" — which, Ching told us, changes its meaning according to the political aims of the time. The Rent Collector's Courtyard was a favourite spot for education during the Cultural Revolution, so none of the students from Chengdu were interested in going — they'd been many times, especially the Party members like Li and Jiang, who were chuckling before we went about the old days, when they'd had to quote sayings from Mao. Their laughter scandalized me a touch. Anyhow, the bus ride was effective Class Education about the peasants now, and the visit to the old landlord's home taught me a lot about their lives before Liberation.

The annual income of the landlord, Liu Wen Cai: $12 million. He had eight other estates besides this one. One wife, five official concubines, 23,000 suits of clothes (are there enough days in a person's life for that many clothes?). A torture chamber and two water dungeons. In the Twenties, he had rents collected 30 years in advance, up until 1953. He bought little girls when their parents couldn't pay their taxes, kept six women giving him breast milk all his life. There was a room for smoking opium.

"Because smoking opium increases your desire, this bedroom was next door. Here Liu Wen Cai tortured many young girls," explained one student. I learned you can still get *one* puff of opium for a bad cough in the countryside for one yuan. Liu Wen Cai died of syphilis, opium addiction and "shock" at the coming Liberation, in 1949, in Chengdu. A landlord, warlord, exploiter, and bandit: "four in one."

There's a famous collection of life-size sculptures depicting the annual payment of rent in the form of grain; there are copies of these statues in Beijing. The scenes are quite harrowing, and I asked about the role of one of the figures who was collecting the bags of grain from the peasants. With some embarrassment, a student said, "Well, we used to call these people 'running dogs'; we always thought that was the proper name in English. What would you call him?" Ian and I were hard put to come up with a better name — we finally settled on "overseer," but not with any real satisfaction.

We were also given a splendid banquet lunch at Da Yi, with the Japanese experts and various honchos. Field eels. Peanuts. Green beans. Pork and mushrooms. Pork and green peppers. Pork and fresh bamboo shoots. "Fried egg flour" with sugar. Wonderful eggplant that I must learn how to make. Chicken soup. *Yuan cai tung*: soup with dumplings. And fancy *mantou* and *mifan* (rice), of course. And ta da! new Pinyin labels for Tsingtao beer: "Qingdao."

I'm very glad we got to go to the Rent-Collector's Courtyard, because a long time ago, during the Cultural Revolution I now realize, I'd pored over a catalogue of the sculpture collection in a bookstore in Toronto.

Monday, June 9
Dear Janet and Douggie and Oliver,

One thing you can forget worrying about instantly is Ian and me gabbling about you in Chinese; we have still barely mastered the rudiments. I have to think hard to say a *number* and we just don't have the time to study between our Chinese lessons. We can have scintillating and deep conversations about you and Penny on the order of "She's a teacher"; "She's Canadian." About the most malicious thing we can manage on any subject is the Chinese equivalent of "no good." One phrase we have become very familiar with (Ian has dubbed it the slogan of the PRC) is *mei you*. This means, literally "no have" and is the typical response to "Do you have any black tea/toilet paper/beer/matches/slippers in my size/ cigarettes/glue/letters for us?" Sort of like *no hay* in Spanish. The reason we need glue — not for sniffing purposes — is because stamps and envelopes are not glued when you buy them. Well, stamps are a *bit*, but the glue's not reliable.

Not speaking of telephones, Doug should have a look at the phones here. They're surprising — plastic things in all sorts of two-toned bright colours (especially in the blue-green range, like light green body and dark green receiver) plus an equal number of the old Thirties black models. You know, no dial! And then there's the experience of making a long-distance call! We've made two phone calls to Beijing to our much less than helpful Canadian Embassy and I was cut off at least six times; much yelling and shouting because you have to speak over the equivalent of a busy signal!

Yesterday we were taken on a tour with some of our students — to the "Rent Collector's Courtyard"; it's an old estate of a pre-Liberation landlord. A multi-millionaire who made his yuan mercilessly gouging the peasants. There's a famous collection of sculptures depicting the yearly payment of grain by the peasants. We had a great time — it involved a three-and-a-half-hour bus ride through the countryside on market day (pigs being driven to market, baskets of ducklings, open-air barbers and thousands of people, staring at us, of course). None of the students from Sichuan came because they'd all seen it, several times. They missed a marvellous banquet, with the local Sichuan specialty:

eels. Blagh! These days, you see people on the streets, gutting eels on a horrifyingly bloody board, their hands red to the wrists with eel blood. I'm a good sport, but I was glad I had my fish allergy to fall back on.

The hot weather's beginning. And the mosquitoes are settling in. So we're getting mosquito netting for around our beds.

Michael Gasster, the American history expert, left last week. I think I'll be moving into his place on the third floor opposite Ian. However, I'll have to check it out carefully before I make any rash decisions — my toilet works like a charm (in my place on the first floor) but the plumbing on the third floor is a horror. Michael woke up to find his bedroom ankle-deep in water one day before he left. Oh, well, I suppose it got a good cleaning that way. The Chinese were astounded to discover that North Americans wash their floors with soap. "We Chinese do not do so."

We're now familiar with some parts of the downtown; and this is a source of pride. Every Saturday we negotiate a few major transactions on our own (like returning a huge pile of beer bottles or getting my bicycle seat fixed), so we're getting cocky.

When we start feeling isolated and bewildered due to lack of news, we either use Pat Parson's shortwave to get the Voice of America or, more frequently, the BBC. Or, what's more fun, we ride our bikes into town to the Jin Jiang Hotel and watch the news on Chinese colour TV.

You asked about a care package. Well, I really miss my J.J. Cale albums and Ry Cooder and Leon Redbone, and other treats like that...

DIARY ENTRY
Tuesday, June 10

"I was speaking to the workers in the kitcl
morning after breakfast," I remarked casually to
the way to dinner tonight.

"Oh?" he said suspiciously, knowing how inc
am of a casual chat in Chinese.

"And they told me what they're making for
dinner tonight."

"What?" Ian inquired.

"Quiche, a spinach salad, and they have som
wine in the fridge for us."

"Ah," he mused, "probably a Chateauneuf de P

"Oh, and I forgot," I continued, *"frites."*

"And for dessert?" he asked. "A little str
tarte?"

"No, apricot. With *crème fraiche*. And cappu
we'd like it."

"Oh, stop it," he moaned.

韓琳

Wednesday, June 11
Dear Mom and Dad,

Well, the days are rushing by faster and faste
ever; the warm weather is coming, not yet really w
We've had a few scorchers, but the next day (
night) the weather cools off remarkably.

We still draw big crowds on the street, and I'
nonplussed by it, but we're slowly but surely
familiar with the city.

We met an Australian woman, Audrey Donnitl
who's doing research on the Chinese economy. Sh
born in Sichuan, not far from Chengdu (missi
parents) and came back to study and teach at Si
University in 1940. She said that there were no car

because "petrol" couldn't be brought in from the coast and there wasn't even a railway. That really astounded us, I guess because building the railway in Canada was the first thing we did. She told us of her journey here in 1940 — by truck and boat and sedan chair, from Guangzhou (Canton); I think that's at least a thousand miles.

On Sunday we took a day trip out about 50 km into the countryside. It took about three hours because it was market day in all the villages and the roads were clogged with people and bicycles, so that the bus crawled and speeded and stopped and crawled. Many near misses. The prevailing attitude on the road, as Ian describes it, is "Everybody has to look out for me, because I'm not looking out for myself." The way people pull out onto the road in front of you would make your hair grey in a matter of minutes. Oh, sorry, Dad — maybe yours would go back to its original colour.

We don't understand why — but we always get all our letters on one or two days a week, and the other days we get none. Maybe just chance. The American expert (who left last week) said it was because the censor was having trouble translating the letters, so he was taking a few days' holiday! I don't think letters are censored, really — apparently incoming letters are sometimes opened in Hong Kong, and anti-Communist propaganda inserted. A *rare* letter arrives opened, but I don't think it's official policy . . .

韓琳

DIARY ENTRY
Thursday, June 12

No mail all week. Not a sausage. *Mei you.*

Reports are flooding in, in the diaries we have our students keep, of the preparations, rehearsing and planning of the "dancing party" the students have been

asked to put on to replace the one at the Physics Department that was so inopportunely cancelled. I am looking forward to this with as little enthusiasm as we are looking forward to our first swimming session at the Chuan Da (Sichuan University) swimming pool. This is because I am horrified at the amount of staring that will, without a doubt, take place. "They told us they change the water once a week, on Sunday," we said to one of Ian's students. "They tell a lie," he replied. That's our second concern about the swimming pool.

The following excerpt, complete with errors, is from one of my students — a description of his unit, which was the topic of a paragraph I assigned. We'd been touching on the theme of "my neighbourhood" in a Canadian short story I did with my class last week.

> I live in an institute, around which are some factories. Most of the people in my neighbourhood are common teachers as I, workers and clerks of the institute. We call the area where we live, "the Third World." Because "the First World," well-equipped apartment, is for the super leaders; "the Second World" is for the cadres of each level. In "the Third World" each room means a family, often two or three generations. The kitchen and toilet there are shared by several families.

And reported in one of Ian's student's diaries was a comment made during our visit to the Rent Collector's Courtyard at Da Yi. The waiting room, where we were given tea and a "brief introduction," was provided at the charge of 20 yuan. One student remarked, "The landlord may be dead, but his spirit lives on."

韓琳

· TEACHERS OF TEACHERS ·

One evening, a short time after we arrived in Chengdu, Ian and I were sitting in my apartment with our interpreter, Jiang, trying to explain our discomfort at how he translated the term *waibin* into English: as "distinguished foreign guest." We suggested he could drop the term "distinguished" in reference to us. Protesting, Jiang replied that we shouldn't feel embarrassed, because, especially as teachers, we were worthy of this respect. He supported his remarks with a quote that amazed me as much for its source as for its content: "As our great leader, Stalin, said, 'Teachers are the engineers of mankind'*; and to be the teachers of teachers — !" Clearly, there were few greater honours.

Stalin's remark on teachers stayed with me the whole time I was in China, because I encountered a daily reminder in my classroom. Each day, as I stood at the front of the room, my

---

*The Westerner in China is often struck by the contradiction between the great respect for Stalin and the mistakes in the Stalinist "China Policy" that Mao only indirectly attributed to Stalin himself. These concerned the importance Stalin placed in the Twenties on the organizing of the Chinese industrial workers over the sector Mao identified as the revolutionary base in China, the peasants, who form eighty per cent of the population. Stalin insisted that the Communist Party remain within Chiang Kai-Shek's Nationalist Party, the Guomindang, even after the GMD turned against the Party and began to massacre its members in 1927. The ultimate Stalinist error was his belief, stated at the Yalta Conference in 1945, that the government of Chiang Kai-Shek was the legal government of China. Despite these insulting, even disastrous policies, the official Chinese evaluation of Stalin in 1963 was that his "achievements are considerable, his errors are venial."

gaze would travel up the back wall to a point about a foot from the ten-foot high ceiling to greet his portrait, along with those of Marx, Engels and Lenin. The Chinese contingent of Mao and Hua Guofeng were placed at the front of the classroom above the blackboard. It didn't take long, a week or two at most, for us to find those stern faces familiar, but my initial thought at seeing them hovering above our classroom activities was to wonder if their presence signalled a merging of politics and learning that had never before seemed possible to me.

Our students took the presence of these socialist thinkers for granted. They did not, however, take for granted the opportunity their colleges were offering in sending them to our training course. They knew they would be under considerable pressure to show their language improvement after the significant investment of time and money their colleges had made in placing them under our foreign expertise. They also knew that when they went back to their own colleges, they would have very little time to prepare the material they would be teaching that year. In addition, many of them felt overwhelmed by the demands of their students, whose English was often as good as theirs. The present crop of undergraduate students had, for the most part, gained admission to the universities by passing a set of rigourous entrance examinations — a condition reintroduced in 1977 — that the teachers themselves had not had to fulfill. During the Cultural Revolution (1966-1976), many students were admitted to the colleges and universities on a political basis. These people, essentially from worker, peasant or soldier backgrounds, now formed a sizeable core of the teaching faculties of the colleges and universities. Our students had lived through the Cultural Revolution as English teachers, through a period when the study of anything foreign was extremely suspect. Many had had to give up even private study of English while they spent time in the countryside, and they resented the "wasted" years when their English had gotten rusty. The fact that they were now being given access to retraining by foreign experts was a recognition that they were indeed ill-equipped for teaching.

Our student teachers suffered from great insecurity over their proficiency in English and were grateful for the training course that, they hoped, would given them an edge on their students.

We had been given *carte blanche* in selecting the content of our course by the leaders of the university. They were, nevertheless, interested in what we were setting out to do, and wanted to be kept informed of the new ideas and texts we would be bringing into the classroom. We were also given complete freedom in our choice of language teaching methods, and it was repeatedly stressed to us that this opportunity for contact with the newest Western techniques was going to be invaluable for our teacher "trainees," as they were called.

Because the *what* and the *how* of our courses had been left up to us, it was startling to encounter the resistance on the part of our students to, primarily, our language teaching methods. We had been prepared to some extent for this by people we knew in Canada who had taught in China. Yet for both Ian and me, it was surprising to find that the preference of our students was not exposure to new methods. They would have loved us to spend one hundred per cent of our time at the front of the classroom, explaining in minute detail the structures of sentences and the meanings of words in a preferably famous text. We both felt very strongly that the role of the language teacher is to get students to practise and perform the broad range of things that we normally do with language. This meant there was a significant divergence between ourselves and our students on the question of the teacher's role in class. They saw us as dispensers of information and knowledge, while we saw ourselves as the agents who concocted and organized activities that would enable them to speculate and analyze and argue — to stretch the boundaries of the English they already had.

Consequently we ran right into a dispute over a "student-centred" versus a "teacher-centred" class, and we were disturbed that the students were so firmly in favour of the more traditional set-up. There were conflicts, too, over the students' best use of their time outside the classroom.

These occurred because of the traditional Chinese emphasis on rigid, disciplined "self-study," including a great deal of memorization and "reading aloud," techniques that have been largely discarded in the West in favour of more spontaneous types of language practice. However, because we recognized the importance of allowing the students to determine their needs, it was essential to be flexible around this question, and, ultimately, for all of us to compromise. From my own experience on the student's side of the desk, I knew that panicky feeling of not learning what I wanted or needed to learn from a course I considered crucial. And certainly, beneath this question of individual preferences in teaching and learning, there was a cultural bedrock of expectations concerning a teacher's role, and, essentially, how people learn. This was another, and probably more significant, level on which the conflict occurred.

It was important for Ian and me to bear in mind as we dealt with these conflicts that it made little sense for us to dismiss the kind of language teaching methods these teachers were accustomed to, as outdated as many of the techniques and preferences seemed to us. For, clearly, it was precisely through these methods that our students had acquired such fluency in English. And I should not neglect to point out, as well, that the intensity of this initial conflict over methods was, in fact, a sign of the deep motivation for language learning that these young teachers had.

It took us several weeks to get a clear idea of the backgrounds of our students, but there were some things about their needs as English teachers that were apparent from our first meeting. Although they had all attained a remarkable command of the language, there was a common weakness in their comprehension of natural spoken English. Another problem was the peculiar form of English that they wrote and spoke: mixed in with the usual, and sometimes amusing, mistakes that all second language learners make ("She was employed in that office as a typewriter"; "The rainballs were falling heavily"; "the story of Adam and Evil") was a peculiarly Chinese usage of English, which had several elements. One was a reliance on out-of-date words and phrases (we were occasionally asked if we owned gramophones; a woman pilot was referred to as an "aviatrix"). Another strand of this problem was the unwitting mix of ordinary, neutral, expository style with a rhetorical style, which produced an exaggerated formality in their writing and speech. Our students considered it impressive to be able to use phrases like "unyielding integrity" and "dogged by misfortune," and to write sentences like "They strengthened their resolve to scale new heights of scientific research." Of course, this was the type of English our students were exposed to in Chinese dictionaries and grammar books and in Chinese-produced English publications like *The Beijing Review*. And we slowly discovered a deeper reason for the Chinese attachment to this style. When we first attacked the kind of writing that struck us as cliché-ridden or trite or far-fetched, our students, puzzled, asked us if we had no respect for tradition. The Chinese appreciate the ability to use well-known phrases that echo famous works of literature; this notion is in direct conflict with our attitude, which values self-expression that is "new" or "fresh" or "original." Ian and I spent countless hours, mostly privately with our students, justifying our distaste for what seemed overly facile and overly formal turns of phrases. Our preoccupation with clichés became a joke with our students, and we began to "ration" their use, restricting our students to one per day!

Another unexpected tendency we encountered in our students' speech was one that, we surmised, resulted from the transfer of the rules of the Chinese language to the rules of English. This was the use of abrupt forms such as "Sit down, please," "Drink tea, please," or "You will now please go inside and wash." These expressions had been taught to our students as correct English; they appeared in textbooks and were heard in their classes all the time. Challenging these curt usages and explaining the English love of indirectness in suggestions to other people ("Why don't you...?"; "If I were you, I'd..."; "Would you like to...?") was a momentous task. In addition to these peculiarities of speech, our students exhibited a studied, unspontaneous conversational style and often missed the turns of a conversation as they silently rehearsed what they were about to say. However one great strength they all shared was an impressive mastery of English pronunciation, which was a credit to their training and to the seriousness with which they approached the new language.

Our students had no formal training in the writing of English, and so had to be given step-by-step instruction in basics like the paragraph and other forms of written English. Their reading abilities, solid at the level of close grammatical and lexical analysis of a text, needed expanding to include skills like skimming a text, analyzing the motives and consequences of a character's actions, and critically judging the author's ideas.

Underlying all these linguistic needs was a problem that Ian and I puzzled long and hard over. This was the fundamental lack of shared information and knowledge about things, events, persons, values and concepts that are the "cement" of our communications with others in our native language. This problem frequently left us sighing over how "culturally bound" many of the materials we had brought with us were. On the first few pages of a magazine article we read dealing with the transformation of former student radicals into present-day managers in North America, I had to explain the following things: three-piece suits, the anti-war movement, the draft, smoking joints, hippies and beads, folk music, the baby boom, the Depression, proms and fraternities, affirmative action, career planning, "moving up the corporate ladder," consumer advocacy, "the little guy," shareholders, life insurance and workaholics. The task of reading a magazine article from the West was rendered amazingly complex by factors that had less to do with language than with life and culture.

We also had to bear in mind that our students were attending this course to improve their skills as teachers, and that it was essential to acquaint them formally and systematically with the understanding we had of the various methodologies of language teaching.

One irritant that plays like a stuck record in these letters and diary entries is my rather ungracious response to the withdrawal of the usual support system that most teachers in

Canada enjoy: easy access to xeroxing or duplication, the availability of resources like books, magazines, games, music and films, the use of reliable and up-to-date audio-visual equipment like film and slide projectors, tape recorders, radios and videotape equipment. All of these were available; it was simply very difficult to arrange to use them, and they were quite frequently not working properly. (A tape recorder that muffles a speaker's words is, I found, more frustrating than no tape recorder at all.) I was envious whenever I heard that an expert at another university was able to have his or her materials duplicated within twenty-four hours; for a host of reasons, we were never able to arrange duplication of our materials in less than two weeks. I would laboriously type out texts and exercises onto wax stencils that were used in the antiquated printing machines in our university, and when the two-week wait for duplicated materials stretched into six or ten, I would write the exercises on the blackboard.

I think precisely because of the scope of our goals and all of these significant difficulties, the small victories our students achieved over the months we worked with them seemed very important. One student confided to me that he never wrote his assignments in English, but did them in Chinese first and then translated them, which was why even a small amount of writing took him so long. With encouragement and some private teaching, he finally broke himself of this habit. It gave us both a lot of pleasure. Discovering a hard core of the students developing an addiction to Scrabble, a game we taught them, was another treat. I would often chuckle, hearing the protests of "Hey! That's not a word!" as I walked into the study room adjoining our office. It was a pleasure, as well, to see the students develop in their writing ability, so that one task we assigned them, the keeping of diaries, became less and less an onerous task, and more and more an enjoyable and intensely personal communication of daily events, feelings and opinions. One student of Ian's, a former Russian teacher, decided to use his diary as a format to write his family history, and he was such an excellent storyteller that he kept us breathlessly waiting for the next installment. My students were startled to realize, because this was progress that they hadn't noticed they were making, that by the end of the course they could understand almost every word I said when I spoke at a normal rate of speech. This certainly hadn't been the case when they began the course.

Finally, there is one all-important factor in any teaching-learning project that must be assessed; and this is the relationship between the teacher and the learners, the atmosphere and rapport that develop between these partners. Just as I had never before experienced such a demanding teaching task, I had also never experienced the degree of warmth and appreciation that evolved between our students and ourselves. They brought with them an enthusiasm and diligence so intense that they frequently exhausted us. But there also developed an intimacy and camaraderie that, I think, resulted from their accepting the responsibility of teaching *us* the language, the culture and politics of China. One of the most delightful signs that things are going as they should in a language classroom is the frequent occurrence of comfortable laughter. And it was especially gratifying to hear the bursts of laughter that resulted from one of Ian's or my misconceptions or gaffes, because these laughs and chuckles meant that the frustrations, insecurities and barriers were melting.

韓琳

Friday, June 13, 1980
Dear Pat,

Well, here's the long-awaited/promised letter. Today is the hottest day to date, a scorcher, and the day we chose to make a clandestine trip into town on our bikes with two students. They wanted to see the inside of the Friendship Store. (It's for foreigners only, government-run, with jacked-up prices; it has everything from bikes to peanuts to carpets. And a lot of kitsch.) These two students are from another city, as most of our students are, and imagine our delight at

- knowing the city better than they do (we took them to "The Café Vienna" for ice cream);

- being able to ride our bikes better than one of them (he's a "beginner"). This shocked us. We thought the Chinese were born able to ride bikes, as women are born able to type! This line of thought is consistent with the Chinese amazement at *our* ability to ride bikes: people who have studied English frequently pedal along beside us asking us as we pedal, too: "Can you ride a bike?" "Non, je n'ai jamais appris," I sometimes respond.

I'm now sitting on Ian's balcony trying not to think about ice cubes, and Ian's plunging his toilet. Ian's apartment has a *lot* of plumbing problems. And no one to fix them. "The workers of our university" as our interpreter calls them, have been asked to come about 75 times. But they never do. The simplest thing takes two weeks to get done, more difficult things (like our request to include Lhasa as one of the cities on our tour at the end) take a century.

I'm experiencing the same difficulty you reported you had when you were teaching in Japan. That is, when people say, "We Chinese do this in this way; how do Canadians do it?" I am unable to give an explanation, because whatever is being discussed — whether it is finding a husband, our attitudes to our parents, making a cup of tea — there are so many different ways of doing each back home. I don't quite know what to do about the expectation that the North American way of doing things is uniform and doesn't vary from class to class and from person to person. It's the same phenomenon as the "We Japanese..." thing you mentioned.

Our teaching is becoming more and more a pleasure. I'm really impressed by our students' kindness, enthusiasm and friendliness. The ones we went out with this afternoon "repaid" us with about two dozen Chengdu peaches, our first of the season. We're very lucky to be here because fruit and fresh vegetables are nearly impossible to get in most big cities in China.

Well, Friday the thirteenth is passing fairly uneventfully in Chengdu — you've heard all the highlights of the day. You won't forget about the two lost souls, will you?

DIARY ENTRY
Saturday, June 14

A "bitter controversy" that affects almost all our students is being reported in their diaries. It's the new national policy announced by the Ministry of Education to give a five to seven per cent salary increase to 40 per cent of the teachers in China. This is the first wage hike for teachers since the Sixties, but that doesn't have as much meaning here as in Canada, since China has not really had any inflation until the last two or three years. Imagine a society where prices and wages stayed the same for almost 20 years.

But how will it be decided which teachers get the raise and which don't? This is what is making everyone nervous. Meetings of all the faculty are being held in each school, and every teacher has to explain why he or she deserves a raise. The other teachers listen to this and then appraise and criticize the individual's eligibility. Finally, after the process has been followed for each teacher in the department, the faculty members vote to produce a list of teachers recommended for a raise. This list is given to the leaders of the department, who make the ultimate decision.

Some of our students, who have been with their departments since the early Sixties, are very discouraged about their prospects of getting a raise. They are still considered "junior" members of their departments because retirement is rare. It makes them angry because they feel they carry the weight of the department.

A beginning teacher usually gets about 48 yuan ($32) a month, compared to the average worker, who gets about 60 yuan ($40); however, I have heard of chairmen of departments getting as much as 350 yuan ($275) a month. The ranks of teachers in a university department are: assistant, lecturer, vice-professor and professor. An assistant teaches both terms every year, while a lecturer usually teaches only one; vice-professors and professors teach either one or two years out of three, to allow them to do research and materials compilation. The new teacher has 12 hours of classes a week, and the scale goes down to eight or six or four, or even two, as you rise up in the ranks.

When I first thought about this salary-raising dispute, I tried to imagine a similar set of negotiations at a college in Canada — inconceivable. I decided that this was a reasonable way to go about giving a raise to teachers in a country that can't afford to give everyone a raise. But then I realized that this method is leaning in the direction of material incentives, and is very consistent with China's "new direction." Of course, so is the fact even of allocating more money for teachers — under Mao, who thought "bourgeois ideas are infused in the blood of the intellectuals," any improvement in their lot would not have been undertaken.

One of my students, who's been feeling some anxiety over the salary-raising dispute, wrote a composition this week, and I was struck by how similar some of his complaints are to ones I've heard in staff rooms in Canada. Some, but not all of his clichés have been removed in correction:

TROUBLES AND WORRIES
IN CHINESE TEACHERS

During the Cultural Revolution, because of the obstruction from the Gang of Four, only the workers, peasants and soldiers were revolutionary elements, while teachers were the targets of the revolution. Schools were taken as the hotbeds of capitalism; teachers were slandered as the tools of revisionism. Many teachers were struggled against, locked up and even killed. But now, things are entirely different. Just like the workers, peasants and soldiers, the teachers are highly respected by the people and the society and they are also looked on as the masters of the country.

Although the teachers have stood up in politics, their economic situation has been less changed. One of the obvious characteristics is that the teachers are rather poor.

Why I should say so is mainly because their salaries are lower than other people's. Compared with an ordinary worker of the same age, in general, a teacher's salary is one-third lower than that of the worker. Besides, the workers enjoy a money award or bonus as well as other material benefits every month. As for teachers, there is nothing for them except their low pay. The factory supplies all the implements of production for the workers yet the teachers have to pay for the teaching books and reference books themselves.

In contrast with the workers, the working time of the teachers are longer. The workers work eight hours a day but the teachers' working time is far over it. Most of the teachers are quite busy and usually keep working till midnight preparing for tomorrow's lesson. If a worker works overtime, he gets overtime pay. As for a teacher, if he works overtime it is considered that he should do so and no one pays him anything.

In other aspects, such as housing conditions, working conditions, the teachers' lives are different from other people. I surmise that is why people are unwilling to be a teacher and to marry the teachers.

Sunday, June 15
Dear Comrade Mom and Comrade Dad,

Dad, I got your magazines, clippings and letter yesterday, and what a treasure! That coverage on Mount St. Helen's was a knockout. We pored over the magazines, and Ian snaffled the *Maclean's* instantly because of the cover story on Mordecai Richler. He'd just done a short story with his class by Richler and they'll be thrilled to see all those pictures of him.

Well, the big event of the week has been moving into the third floor flat. It *is* hotter, but brighter and airier, and has a balcony, so that I can open the balcony door and the front door and get a nice breeze. Also, my bedroom is off the balcony so it's pleasant for sleeping. Our mosquito nets were installed yesterday, and now I have the closest thing to a four-poster bed I think I'll ever have. The nets make the bed look quite pretty.

I guess the hot weather's beginning. It was 31°C yesterday and people told us that this is about the hottest it ever gets, with an occasional rise to 33°C or even 35°C. That's not bad; I can take that. It's very humid, though. We've been promised electric fans, but they're amazingly expensive (80 to 100 yuan or $60 to $85).

This is Sunday morning and we were going to sleep in (ahh!) but I woke up with a start at 7:30 thinking I was late for breakfast (it's at 7:15, but we managed to cancel breakfast in our terrible Chinese). I guess sleeping in my new place made it easier for me to hear the loudspeakers and activity in the courtyard. This morning we had "The Sound of Music" in Chinese blaring out over the university community...

DIARY ENTRY
June 15

As I write this, there are disturbingly real crowd noises thronging into my open windows, and I can't quite make out if it's a real crowd, or the usual inconsiderate neighbour who's got his TV on so loud I can't think. Who *is* this person who owns a TV and who so mercilessly inflicts it on the entire courtyard? Oh, well, the nightly TV tumult has at least two favourable consequences: it makes me feel less guilty about typing late into the night, and it makes it less shocking for the leaders that we sometimes want to go to the hotel to get our work done (but TV is an omnipresent energy — they have one there, too). The noise in China, generally, is a *big deal*; it is one of the factors in our ongoing culture shock. I frequently can't play tapes in class because we can't hear them, even at top volume, over the noise outside the classroom. And when I do play a tape, all the students have to leave their seats and crowd around my desk to catch the words.

Monday, June 16
Dear Carolyn and Michael,

I keep thinking of you two a lot because I keep getting all these reminders: one is the urgently-needed mosquito coil glowing at my right and producing just a little more heat on a sweltering night. Another is my desperate need for a Pointee-Talkee book. Michael could make a tidy sum by producing a phrase book for *waiguo ren*; I'm serious about that — and I could organize it according to the needs such a foreigner has. Another reason is that people keep sending me pictures of you, Carolyn. Betty O'Brien has been saving our lives by sending us a weekly batch of clippings. That's how I got that great picture of the International Women's Day Committee's "Take Back the Night" demonstration.

So the weather's changed — we've gone from nippy fall-like weather to hot, "close," humid stuff. (I thought the only person who described a humid day as "close" was my mother — but our students, in their best formal English, kindly inquire, "Are you feeling closed?")

One symptom of our culture shock, our debilitating exhaustion, is gradually clearing up. It's just plain *wearing* to be constantly trying to figure out what's going on. Lots of unwritten laws.

For example, everyone gets on and off her/his bicycle in a certain way. This is called The Chinese Way; other ways are called "stupid" or, slightly better, "ridiculous." Of course we get on and off our bikes The Stupid Way. Actually I must admit The Chinese Way looks a lot more graceful. Perhaps I'll be able to demonstrate both when I get back. The extent to which this society is organized around bicycles still floors me, although I thought I knew about it before I came. The traffic is harrowing, and that's a mild word, but there's something very peaceful about moving in unison with hundreds of cyclists on a long stretch of Chengdu's lovely tree-lined streets — it's the intersections that have been developing my reflexes.

We finally got an NFB Catalogue from the Embassy. The Embassy, by the way, is not the most helpful of organizations. We have been here seven weeks and they've sent us one eight-minute film. The people who were at Guangzhou in previous years got a film a week. I know we're in the boonies, but!

There's been a ban on foreign films in language classrooms; it's affected some German teachers in Nanjing and our Canadian friends in Guangzhou. But not here. The leaders keep hungrily asking me when the Canadian films are coming.

Things in the classroom are just fine, especially as we get to know our students. They work killingly hard and are very receptive to our ideas, ever since we compromised on the war about spending all of our time in the classroom explaining the reading texts (boring, useless — they can read perfectly well, but need lots of listening and speaking). This Friday night we're taking the students from Guizhou province out to dinner in a restaurant. This is something all concerned are looking forward to.

Something I'm *not* looking forward to is a "dancing party" that's being organized to console us for the cancellation of the first one. Ever since the downfall of the Gang of Four, we've been carefully told, all the old customs that the Chinese people used to enjoy are slowly beginning to be permitted again. Dancing is one: a former "decadent, bourgeois, wasteful" activity. The students have been practising (and learning) ballroom dancing one or two nights a week. There are exactly two people in our two groups (33 total) who can dance (one learned before Liberation: he's a delightful man, and like plenty of older teachers, is a recycled Russian teacher, now teaching English after 20 years of Russian teaching) and they are helping everyone else get ready for this event. I shudder at the thought. I've repeatedly told them about my "two left feet" (they love clichés) but they think it's humility. I'm the one who should be practising, but I'm keeping busy learning The Chinese Way of getting on a bike.

Before I forget, I want to ask if there is anything in particular you people would like from here. Not that there's much to choose from (some peanuts? a nice mirror in the shape of a swan? some plastic sandals? a spittoon?). Really, don't hesitate to mention something you'd like because our students love helping us out in doing this kind of thing.

Marsha wrote and told us her father would like an Einstein stamp that was issued a couple of months ago. So we went to four different post offices and managed to inquire about it, but *mei you* ("no have"). A few days later, a student brought us one. Plenty of generous things like that have happened.

Well, all the lights are out except for a certain foreign teacher's. Even the mosquito coil has gone out; I guess it's time for me to crawl into my newly mosquito-netted bed. The net is a necessity. Chinese mosquitoes are quicker than Canadian ones. Good night...

June 16
Dear Julie and Tom and Bas and Theo,

Well, time's going by slowly and quickly at the same time — the weeks are mounting up, but we still think the weekdays crawl along till the weekend comes. *That's* the same as being at home.

Being here is a mixture of the unassimilable and the dull. Some of the unassimilable things: harrowing bicycle traffic, constant spitting, very heavy schedules, numerous smelly dung carts being pulled from the city to the countryside by peasants, the noise, the heat. Since we're into a set routine things *do* get a bit dull, but we liven them up by riding into town on our bikes for a *cold* beer at the hotel. Ian, formerly not a beer lover, has acquired a taste for the wonderful Chinese beer. Oh, I'm afraid the language is unassimilable, too!

The kids here are adorable — and I'm constantly trying to figure out the games they're playing. There are two three-year-old girls who do a Chinese version of "I'm a little tea-pot" (add politics, I guess) each evening in our courtyard. Little boys play hide and seek, marbles, a kind of card game played with old cigarette packages, and a game where you hop around on one leg trying to knock down the other hoppers. I even saw one little boy running a hoop down the street with a stick! I'd never seen one of those except in illustrations in my own children's books.

In fact, many things that we've forgotten about are in use here — electric set-ups to give you a permanent in the barber's/hair dresser's. This is the more expensive kind of perm; the cheaper kind is done with chemicals. Ian got a Chinese haircut (I took photos) and it was hilarious. The barber said he could comb *my* hair "into a flower." I'm going to try it one time, but I'm not sure it'll really be me...

DIARY ENTRY
Tuesday, June 17

A phrase that has become common between Ian and me: "A five-yuan fine, depending on your attitude." This is how we scold each other for minor breaches of etiquette and inadvertent bloopers. The source of this was finding out that it is forbidden to litter in movie theatres — *after* Ian had taken peanuts with him when we went to see *The Red Shoes* (with Moira Shearer, dubbed in Chinese). He shared them all around and also left a mound of shells behind him. Generally, there is not a great deal of consciousness about littering, so when we discovered that he could have been fined for this transgression, we were horrified. But my students assured me that our attitudes were good, so we wouldn't have been fined anyway. There is also a fine for carrying someone on the back of your bike in traffic; you can get away with it on campus, though.

And, on the subject of *The Red Shoes*, one of my students who wanted an English name, Susan, recorded these amazing conclusions in her diary:

> Last week, we saw a colour movie, *The Red Shoes*, which was produced in Britain: I enjoyed every minute of it and sympathized with the heroine. After seeing the movie, someone said, "The movie is a good example of love destroying fame." But I think there is a close connection between love and fame. If the heroine had got married much later, about 50 years old, she would have gained both love and fame. Now, my family life is a good

reason for my viewpoint. I am an English teacher and my husband is a teacher of physics. We have been helping each other in our work and study ever since we fell in love with each other. He often learns English from me, and I learn something about natural science from him. As my mother-in-law is taking very good care of our baby boy, we needn't worry about him. So we just work, study and walk after supper as usual. Life for us is very happy, and we are sure we'll be successful in our careers.

Wednesday, June 18
Dear Mary Ellen, Nina and Wendy,

Lots of thanks for all the correspondence, errands and concern for the fellow Foreign Language Hotshots in Chengdu. Ian is busy setting up our second shrine (the first is to our bicycles) in honour of the Canadian comrades in Guangzhou. We'll stud it with maple leaf lapel pins, of which we have an abundance.

The duplicating fluid has not, sigh, arrived from Beijing, although we got a letter acknowledging our letters, phone calls and telegrams. They said it would be arriving soon — they'd sent it by slow train (is there anything else?). But that was a week ago. I'm beginning to think of our duplicating machine as one of those, whaddyacallem, Bennett buggies, the cars that were pulled by horses during the Depression because there was no gas.

We're sick to death of hearing about the referendum. We can't complain to anyone in Canada about this because people have generously been sending wads of clippings on all the "federalist back-slapping." After all, we asked for it! But we know you'll understand if we complain to you.

Life continues dully. Our high spirits ebbed noticeably during our illnesses and I was afraid they'd never return; aggravations set in — a series of frustrating events with our living conditions. We got short-tempered and impatient and had no one to take it out on. Our mail dropped off. We got tired of the food. We felt hard done by. We dreamed of ice cubes. I still can't believe that one of the things I asked you to get us in Hong Kong was Ajax (but I don't regret it!). Again, you're getting privileged information — we concealed our discouragement from the people back home. But you, fellow experts, will understand these ups and downs perfectly.

Ah, but every time we jump on our bikes and take a harrowing ride into the Jin Jiang Hotel, have a cold beer and miss about 16 visitors while we're out, we clap each other on the back for the excellent idea, and our spirits are restored. The Jin Jiang isn't a bad place, but as Ian mentioned, not open till 7 in the evening so we feel we're doing something clandestine. (We were told *never* to go off campus after dark. We openly refused to comply.) It's peculiar to feel naughty when you're 32 years old. I'd forgotten what it's like, and I still feel the same perverse pleasure I did when I was a kid! Sometimes we get back as late as 10:30. Wicked.

Especially looking forward to your visit, Mary Ellen. I've moved into a new flat that's much nicer, opposite Ian. The extra bedroom's all set up, sort of (no mosquito nets, yet). I prevented them carrying the extra bed away when they were putting up the frame for the mosquito nets because I couldn't imagine ever being able to get it brought back for your visit. I think that was excellent judgement on my part. So, two nights or longer is just fine; and we'll try to borrow a bike so we can go into town to (a) "the Café Vienna" (b) "Les Deux Magots" and (c) the hotel. Our favourite haunts. Les Deux Magots — another expert-inspired nickname — has a younger crowd.

The telegrams you've been sending about your fruitless efforts to get us duplicating fluid in Hong Kong have been exciting events. Again, many thanks for all the trouble you went to. Hope the heat in Guangzhou isn't killing you (dead bats in your swimming pool, ech!).

Thursday, June 19
Dear Nancy,

Another gruelling day in the life of a certain Foreign Language Expert. First of all, there's no electricity today. Then there's no water. Not a drop. The two women caretakers gave us two sheets to replace our old ones; the new ones are postage stamp size whereas the old ones were perfectly adequate. Two bic pens I brought from Canada stopped working even though there's still ink in them. We spent the afternoon answering the following types of question: "Which is better: '*Can* you speak English?' or '*Do* you speak English?' "; "What's the difference between *improve* and *improve on*, between *agree with*, *agree on* and *agree to*?" Just as I was writing this last sentence, my new pen rolled off the balcony and fell three stories below.

But that's nothing compared to what happened to Ian. Although I've had my share of difficulties with the plumbing in China, Ian's come out from behind to win the Toilet Seat Award for endurance in trying circumstances. His toilet has never worked right (the tank looks like a computer would look if you or I had to hook it up) and the workers keep promising to come and then don't come, or come and botch it up further.

They actually came today. They decided Ian needed a new toilet bowl (as I said, the problem was in the tank), so that's what they installed. The two caretakers, who are described by our interpreters as typical products of the Cultural Revolution, that is, "lazy," had the responsibility of disposing of the *old* toilet bowl. So they threw it out the window. Now one toilet bowl lies in the weeds in the back courtyard, three stories below us.

Of course we're lucky to *have* Western toilet bowls!

Friday, June 20
Dear Betty and Colm,

The big news this week is that we're going to have a holiday! A five-day trek up Mount E Mei, which is a local sacred Buddhist spot, complete with shrines and Buddhist monasteries where we'll spend the nights, no meat, according to Buddhist vegetarian regime (which will be a welcome change since we're given too much meat). There are still monks on the mountain. We're going with our students and they've given us tips — bring warm clothes and food for the monkeys! Apparently the monkeys "play tricks" on visitors. I really hope we see some. So we'll spend July 1, simultaneously celebrating Canada Day and the founding of the Communist Party of China on a mountain, where it's cool, and there are no mosquitoes. No work, no heat, no meat, no mosquitoes — what a treat!

For our ten-day trip at the end, we are allowed to request four cities. We chose Beijing (where we fly out of, to Tokyo; the choice was Beijing or Shanghai), Xian (where the big life-size recently-found ancient statues are), Kunming and *Lhasa*. Ever since we made our request, everyone, but everyone has been trying to dissuade us of this last choice. We've been arguing that if it's good enough for P.E. Trudeau, it's good enough for us.

We met an American photographer last week who'd been giving a photography show all over China (he'd done 27 lectures for different places here) and he had just been given permission to go to Lhasa. He'd been refused four times previously!

Your tapes are well-appreciated. At least, one of them is. *The Manhattan Transfer* (of course one of our two or three real favourites) got chewed up in my shitbox, which was made in shitland, the mythical country that produces only defective equipment. Ian brought a good supply of tapes along, too, so we have some variety. They're saving our lives. Sometimes we do a song for listening practice in class. So far we've done "Maybe Baby" (Buddy Holly);

"You've Got a Friend" (Carole King) — a *big* hit; "You Can't Hurry Love" (Supremes); and Ian's done "Birds Do It" (Eartha Kitt). Next I'm gonna do the Beatles, whom no one had heard of, "Yesterday." Not a bad cross-section, huh?

DIARY ENTRY
Friday, June 20

I'm noting with amusement the consequences of a correction I tried to make gently and discreetly. I'd noticed in several diaries and compositions the phrase "make love" used in what I think is an out-of-date way: for example, "Sometimes, walking in the parks or along the riverbanks, you can see young couples walking along, making love to each other." I puzzled about a suitable phrase to replace it with — "whispering sweet nothings"? The students would *love* that cliché! Finally, after ignoring it, I decided I really should explain what the current meaning of "to make love" is. I explained that it used to mean "courting," but that it was now one of the very few nice expressions we have in the English language to refer to sexual activity. Today, in one of the students' diaries, is an account of the fierce argument taking place in the dormitories over whether or not I am correct!

Saturday, June 21
Dear Mom and Dad,

I've been wracking my brains for something I could send you for your birthday, Dad, but because choices here are really limited, I've decided the nicest thing would be a big long letter.

We're sitting in the bar at the local hotel called the Jin Jiang; the "bird's eye view of Chengdu" in the picture book that I sent you was taken from its roof. It's the tallest building in Chengdu — nine stories.

The bar's air-conditioned (whew!) and has *cold* Tsingtao beer. When the Germans were trying to colonize a part of China in the 19th century, they settled in Tsingtao (a luxurious resort city with beaches, roughly in the area near Shanghai) and built what every German needs, a brewery. Tsingtao's the best beer in China, not generally available to the Chinese, and it's up there with Heineken. And if you gave me a choice of an Ex or a Blue or a Tsingtao, I'd take a Tsingtao.

Speaking of Germany, we've just created an uproar with the staff here in the bar trying to find out who's playing a soccer semifinal with China. After much dictionary-consulting, one of the waitresses came up with "Allemagne." But I doubt that we'll be able to follow any of it. Perhaps someone will consent to telling us the score when it's over. Of course I'm rooting for China.

You asked a lot of questions about our teaching in the second last letter, so I'll try to answer them. Our students would spend 24 hours a day with us if they could. They want to learn everything. They have varied backgrounds because they're various ages — 24 to 51. The big event in *all* their lives was the Cultural Revolution (1966 to approximately 1976), when formal classes in universities and middle schools were suspended in order for the students to do political work. Some of our students were young students at university then, and some were already teachers. The ones who were teachers were sent to the countryside to receive "re-education" from the peasants for one to seven years and of course, they weren't allowed to teach English. They taught music or art or Chinese literature if they taught at all. The ones who were students at the time, or many of them, became "Red Guards." So the students had their schooling interrupted, and the teachers their teaching experience interrupted. All this didn't last the whole ten years, but all of our "trainees" blame the Cultural Revolution for all the ills in their lives and all the ills in China — the fact that they feel their English isn't very good; the fact that China's behind the Western world in production — everything.

This morning we went with them to the Sichuan brocade factory (there's a picture of it in the brochure I sent you). I was prepared for a dangerous, dirty factory but it was quite clean and appeared very safe. All the new looms are electric — but it was very noisy of course. After some of the things I've seen elsewhere here (jagged pieces of glass for windows on the buses), the factory was impressive.

Well, the soccer's game over (a 2-2 tie) and the bar's closing. Everyone's mopping up the floor.

In the next letter, Dad, I'll draw you a diagram of how Ian's and my toilet tanks are hooked up (not the same). There's a great reliance on rusty wire to keep things together. I've had my share of plumbing difficulties, but Ian's picking up some expertise in two new fields: plumbing and cleaning, as a result of incidents of toilet overflow. We may not be picking up much Chinese, but we sure are getting good at mopping floors.

Well! I'm running out of steam and there's a long dusty ride back to the university so I'd better sign off.

DIARY ENTRY
Sunday, June 22

After the dinner with our Guizhou students on Friday night, we came back to my place and I served about a million cups of tea. We all sat crowded into my place and I pumped everyone about their experiences in the Cultural Revolution.

I asked the ones who had been Red Guards it they had gone to Beijing to be received by Mao, and indeed, most of them had. The youngest student in the crowd very slyly asked, "Were you moved to tears?" and the young woman who had been talking about being sent to Beijing in the first of the eight batches of Red Guards (quite an honour) answered, "Of course, yes, of course I was moved to tears," a bit nettled. I asked how Mao had received them — from a viewing stand? No, she explained, he had been driven by in a jeep, and the same young student interjected, "Waving his arms like a saint!" but he was ignored that time. I asked if Mao had addressed them, and they replied that he had said a sentence at most, but that Zhou En-Lai had spoken. Yes, they said with slight smiles when I asked, Lin Biao was there, too. We asked where they had stayed, and they said that room was found for them to sleep either in dormitories attached to the university or in parks. After staying in Beijing, they were allowed to take part in the famous movement of youth travelling free by train all over the country — really an unparalleled opportunity for any Chinese — to continue the task of education and struggle in the rest of the country. The purpose of this work was to attack the Soviet-style revisionism within the Party structure in the places they visited.

This student was fifteen when she was greeted by Mao, and I figured out that this was in 1966. She said there were a *million* Red Guards in Tien An Men Square that day!

Later: here's an uncorrected extract from one of my students' diaries on the subject of the dinner:

> Yesterday evening when we're about to leave the restaurant, Maureen presented a souvenir badge [a Canada pin] to an old man of the restaurant [the man who'd served us] and thanked him for his work. The old man asked me whether he could receive the gift. I replied, "Of course you can." It seemed the Chinese would act with caution. Because receiving a gift from a foreign guest was not allowed before. If you did, you should hand it in.

Shades and remnants of the Cultural Revolution mentality, with its severe distrust of corrupting foreign influence.

Monday, June 23
Tomorrow is Miss Li's birthday
Dear Penny,

I'm probably infuriating the entire courtyard by starting this so late, but let's hope they think the foreign expert is killing herself with work into the wee hours. Your letter was a delight; we were dying of laughter over our spicy food at dinner.

We have a new friend! An American woman, whom we moved heaven and earth to try to meet (it took three weeks for our dinner invitation to get to her). She teaches at Chengdu University of Science and Technology — the campus is right behind ours. She's from all over the States, and is a high energy type. She's a vegetarian, she cooks her own food, *makes* cheese, has Chinese friends, is here for two years, but wants to sign up for another two, can manage in Chinese, teaches a million hours a week (what foreign expert doesn't?) and socializes with her students and entertains them by giving them dinner, etc. Oh, she's 29 years old. I'm glad we've made contact with her; she'll maybe inspire me with new energy.

This is going to sound very Partyline or something, but I think the most cheering thing about this whole experience is the contact with the students, and that's the same as any teaching job. I wrote Marsha about taking our students out to a restaurant. (I had the brilliant idea of dividing them up by province, and so we started this series of entertainments with the students from Guizhou [gweyjow] — the Newfoundland of southwest China.) It was wonderful. We plied them with *pijiu*, they forced food into us, and Ian and I even did some singing (note that the level of sobriety generally took a plunge) — something that we've been courteously side-stepping since we arrived. It's true that once we jived for a group of students visiting and another time we sang "O Canada," but that hardly counts. We did some walking after dinner, à la Ian, but had to hurry to catch the last bus — at 9 o'clock! And then we invited them into my place and sat around drinking tea, and I forced a blow-by-blow account out of each of them about what they were doing in the Cultural Revolution. They willingly complied. Several of them had been Red Guards. The line among my leftie friends back home is of course that the campaign against the Cult Rev right now is all part of the rightward trend in China, so I presented that viewpoint as discreetly as possible. They all admitted that Mao (about whom everyone makes nasty cracks) had had the right idea in kicking off the Cult Rev, but that it had "gotten out of control," and then came out all the stories of the fighting, deaths and suicides. This is the most fascinating part of being here; but it's still weird — wherever I am, Canada or China, I feel I have to monitor my political thoughts and not say the brash things I *really* want to blurt out.

Your words about coming back fat(ter) have been duly noted. I'm afraid bicycle riding is not going to do the trick alone. The trouble is, there's so much that we miss that we tend to try to make it up at the table with the things we love, that is, the fattening things. Don't think we're pining away for our homes — what we miss are sort of abstract things like privacy, self-sufficiency, free time. (Hmm. This sounds worse.) There's the other lifestyle and culture rushing in to take the place of the things we miss, but the problem is we don't understand it. Hmm again. I'm going to abandon this train of thought, derailed as it is. The story is, we indulge ourselves a lot, when we can.

Well, the courtyard is stirring from its afternoon nap and we have to go back to the department for our office hours. Thanks a multi-million for managing everything from the Toronto end, tapes and pix and all.

韓珠

DIARY ENTRY
Tuesday, June 24

"Little boys all over the world know how to climb trees," remarked Ian last night as we walked through the courtyard and saw one being scolded for just that. Then today in class we somehow got onto the topic of childhood naughtiness, and I encouraged the students to reminisce about the harmless things they all did and got punished for: using soy sauce to "gamble" (I lost a cup of soy sauce?); burying your younger brother's shoes in the sand and then not being able to find them; going swimming "like an adult" and then finding your clothes gone; fleeing your mother's wrath by jumping into the river where you knew she wouldn't pursue you; sneaking some of your father's wine; running out on the street — we chuckled about the commonalities. And then there was unanimous agreement that parents no longer punish their children so severely because of the One Birth Movement. Now parents spoil their only child, the students told me, amused. I am very slowly beginning to understand the tremendous ramifications of this huge social experiment.

I forgot to ask the woman students if they'd ever climbed a tree when they were kids.

韓珠

Sunday, June 29
Dear Betty and Colm,

Imagine my astonishment last Friday afternoon when I came home, unlocked my door and found an opened *Globe and Mail* pushed under my door, as if for all the world a delivery boy (or girl!) had put it there. No envelope, no name, just the front section of the *Globe*. No letter, so I didn't know who it was sent by. I'll assume it was you, Betty, since you're the only one who sends *Globe* sections; but I imagine you didn't just put an unwrapped, unaddressed *Globe* in the mail and hope it would reach me in China. I know our mail gets opened sometimes, but this is ridiculous! Often the stamps on the letters are missing because there are greedy stamp collectors everywhere. Usually we get our mail at the Foreign Language Department.

Actually, Colm, that reminds me: every time my mail is yanked out of my hands by my students, the stamps carefully removed and the letter handed back to me, I've thought I should ask a George Brown teacher or two or three to ask their ESL classes to bring in a few stamps from their countries and get a wad of them for the people here. If you ever got around to doing that, it would be an incredible windfall for the students here. They so rarely see a stamp from outside China that they go nuts when they do see one.

We've made another American friend, a woman teaching at Chengdu Science and Technology University right behind us. She invited our students and ourselves to an "English Evening" that she'd organized with her students. What a hit! Our students loved every minute, and we were quite impressed with her organizational skills. And her performance. (She was of course the main attraction for the audience.) She'd translated two popular Chinese songs and sang them in Chinese and English. Many cries of "More!" and wild applause. Something that never fails to amaze (and irritate) me is that when what's going on onstage doesn't take the audience's interest, there's so much talking that you can't hear the performance; we couldn't imagine a singer beginning a song in the hubbub, but begin *and* continue they do, despite the talk drowning them out. Except for Sharon's performances and their hilarious "Cinderella" skit (featuring two Chinese-of-course males done up in incredible makeup as the two "sistiuglers": scene-stealers) there was no polite silence or applause. To compound the irony — there was a huge fight (verbal) at the door because not everyone who wanted to come in could, yet no one inside was listening to the show.

So the glove, or shall I say, the mitt, has been thrown to us: Chengdu University and Sichuan University are great rivals since the days of the Cultural Revolution and now *we* have to put on a show!

Any ideas? Can you picture me singing to an audience of 1500 Chinese people? I'm the person the nuns used to tell to "mouth the words" in the choir! We need some ideas of good, rousing, come-all-ye types that are easy and clear, preferably one or two that could be acted out. We've got some ideas, and two songbooks, but any suggestions would be welcome. These are the songs most Chinese students of English know: "Red River Valley," "Ole Black Joe," "Auld Lang Syne," "Oh Susanna," "The More We Get Together" and "Jingle Bells"! That's it. If it wouldn't kill you, I'd love the words to "The Patriot Game" and "The Old Triangle." I hope this isn't a gigantic chore!

The weather's getting hotter and hotter, but, as the *Guidebook to China* says, with "abundant rainfall." It often remains muggy after the rain, too. And I'm not used to it being so hot while it's raining. Oh, no! It just thundered again!

Thanks again for all the correspondence and reading material.

DIARY ENTRY
Tuesday, July 1

Today, Canada Day, and the 57th anniversary of the founding of the Communist Party of China, is perhaps a fitting day to record the big stirrings of rage in my students' diaries over the less-than-selfless behaviour of one of the Party members they've had dealings with lately. It amounted to the fact that this Party member was asked, as a favour, to temporarily vacate the small room in the dormitory she had so that another student whose wife was visiting could use it. When she refused, a small deputation went to her to make her see the situation more sympathetically, in the light of the other student's "three difficulties":

- that this student and his wife are assigned to different units in their own province, and so live apart, and have only their vacations to live together. And of course, his vacation this year is occupied with the training course here;
- that it took this man's wife "four or five days and more than her monthly income to come here for two weeks to be with her husband";
- that the student is in poor health — he has been fighting off a bout of hepatitis since the course started.

There has been a lot of indignation over this woman's refusal to accommodate the couple; one student observed:

> According to the Party Constitution, the Chinese Communist Party consists of progressive elements of the proletariat, and a Party member must be the first to endure any hardship and the last to enjoy himself/herself. But during the Cultural Revolution, a large quantity of disqualified people joined the Party, conceiving the idea that being a Party member would enable one to become an official. This visibly damaged the Party's prestige. Now this kind of behavior makes us see clearer how "ill" the Party is, and we worry more about our country which is always dogged by misfortune.

The indignation has not, of course, been unanimous; one student wondered why this student hadn't arranged something long ago instead of waiting till his wife arrived.

A small incident, and, I suppose, plenty of gossip; but it reflects as much on the "living conditions" in the dormitories as on the Party. All the students feel crowded and uncomfortable in their return to student dormitory life.

Wednesday, July 2
Dear Mary Ellen,

Hope you passed Canada Day in the proper spirit — glugging Labatt's on your back lawn in Guangzhou.

The box of Hong Kong goodies arrived on Friday — and many thanks. The stylish collapsible cotton sun hat will be especially useful; I was trying to figure out what I could use as a hat. The Hong Kong version of Ajax was pressed into immediate service, for our bathtubs.

The plans for Mount E Mei are all up in the air, as I suppose a mountain should be. The dates were announced as "settled" for June 28 to July 2. Then, as the 28th approached, we were told (students and us) that the Foreign Affairs office of the province *hadn't* given permission. Then a few days later, the F.A. office delivered its permission for us to go on *the very dates* that you're coming. We threw tantrums — to the tune of "Out of the 20 weeks we're here, we asked not to have anything like this planned for *one!*" etc.

Back to the drawing board for the dates; but then the leaders informed the students that they were each going to have to *pay* 20 yuan for the trip (this was the first time any money had been mentioned). This is half a month's salary for most of them! They said the leaders had told them they would ask their colleges for reimbursement; that really cheesed them off since their colleges have already paid 200 yuan each for them to take this course.

We're in the middle of all this.

But don't worry — we shall stand firm and steadfastly refuse to leave Chengdu during the period July 15 to 20. We shall serve you Head and Shoulders with cough syrup. We've also found a new place to take you. We call it the "Round Room" à la Eaton's College Street. You can have your ears cleaned there, too.

Still no duplicating fluid — do you believe it? Week ten of our 20-week stay. But four films arrived, which we're showing as fast as possible, both so we can get more soon and to avoid the ban falling down on us before we've shown them all. One thing that arrived, with great fanfare, from the Canadian Embassy was a 20 kg box — goodie! We thought it was the fluid! No, after sending our interpreter downtown to pick it up, we found it was a box full of French publishers' catalogues. *Very* handy! Even if we were teaching French, there wouldn't be the slightest use for them.

I can just see the headlines in the *Globe*: "Foreign Experts in China Form Guerrilla Band Whose Avowed Purpose is to Destroy Canadian Embassy in Beijing."

We're waiting for you with bells on. Bicycle bells.

DIARY ENTRY
Friday, July 4

I've been doing something here that I always intended to do in my teaching, but for some reason, have never gotten around to. That's jotting down the errors that my students make, the ones that make me chuckle. These come mostly from their diaries and compositions.

"On Friday night, Maureen and Ian invited us to a bumper dinner."

"Most of the Chinese, living in a shut-the-door society..."

"At the banquet, we had some bottles of Tsingtao pale ale and a bottle of Tunghua red wine made of wild grapes. They are famous booze in our country and are of high quality."

"We can divide people into two types — those who are time-conscious, and those who are time-unconscious."

"...people who could no longer work owing to cripplehood..."

"The 'Watervalve Incident' is still freshening in our memory. In that incident, Richard Nixon had to resign his President."

Saturday, July 5
Dear Janet,

We got your nice card ("this old town seems pretty blue...") and your second batch of magazines this week, and we slobbered over the prospect of roast lamb at Carolyn and Tom's and marvelled at your faithfulness in writing.

Now let's see: the trip to Mount E Mei has been postponed for the third time, or is it the fourth? The students have to *pay* (this was sprung on them two days ago). This made us feel terrific. But they'll go at any price since, as they explained, they get so few chances to travel. So they got their required "kuai" (yuan) collected and then were told the trip had to be postponed because a bridge had been flooded out. (There were heavy rains last weekend. And I mean *heavy*.)

One thing that annoys me about all this is that the E Mei thing is scheduled for a weekend, is cancelled on Thursday or Friday and then another weekend flashes by, without any sightseeing scheduled. We're not getting to see even the famous sights tourists see in their two-or three-day visits here. We've asked many times to go to the Sichuan opera, but deaf ears.

The other event in our exciting lives was that an Australian journalist, Tony Walker, looked us up on his visit to Chengdu. He was thrilled to be invited to our dining hall for lunch (the equivalent of "Oh? You're in Toronto? How about meeting in the cafeteria at school?"), thrilled to be invited back to our flats to have tea, thrilled with the Tsingtao beer (which he said was hard to get in Beijing).

Well, it's 12:30 on a beautiful Saturday morning, and I think Ian's still sleeping — I don't want to wake him but we have so few days that are sunny but not roasting; we also have so few sleep-in mornings! What to do? I've been puttering around since 10 — we found some *real* coffee in a department store last weekend, and so one lunch hour this week I rigged up a coffee-maker with the aid of a can opener and a hammer: a tin can with holes punched in the bottom to simulate a dripolator. I had a cup of that this morning. Not bad. But I think we should try buying a pot and rigging up a cloth strainer.

Our Chinese remains abominable. Every time we take a tiny leap forward, the comrades in the kitchen, post office, F.L. department all assume we've acquired sudden fluency and begin to talk circles around us. I would be happy with pidgin Chinese, but even that remains beyond my grasp.

Well, I'd better decide what to do with the day ("Foreign Experts Sleep Life Away" reads the headlines in the *Chengdu Daily*).

韓琳

DIARY ENTRY
Sunday, July 6

Tang, a student in my class, put two entries in his diary that set me chuckling when I read them:

> Last night when I woke at four, I heard Comrade Chang talking in his sleep. It seemed to me that he was quarreling in English with somebody. When I woke up, I tried to remember what he had been arguing about, but I couldn't recall. Then I told Chang about it and added that he was a good comrade. Even when he goes to sleep, he still speaks English in his dreams.

And then there was his account of the announcement of the date we were to go to E Mei (again postponed):

> While we were having our class, I saw Ian walking into our classroom on tiptoes, for fear of being seen by Maureen. Then he stood behind her without speaking, smiles on his face. I wondered why he was so glad today. He smiled and nodded at us, and we did nothing but grin till Maureen finally noticed him. He told Maureen the good news about E Mei, and from their expressions we could see that they were very excited, especially Ian. It was very natural for them to feel that way, because E Mei is a very beautiful place which they have been eager to visit for a long time.

韓琳

· BLACK CAT, WHITE CAT ·

One rainy Saturday morning, before our first month in China was over, Miss Li informed me in a very Biblical turn of phrase that "all the instruments and recreations for this afternoon and evening are to be stopped" in order to give everyone a chance to watch a nationally-televised ceremony in Beijing. The ceremony was to be in honour of Liu Shaoqi, who had held the position of president of China, and who had subsequently died in prison, a disgraced man. So, that May afternoon, I rode my Shanghai bike over to the movie theatre on campus, where four colour televisions were set up for the occasion, and, with hundreds of other members of our university unit, watched the rehabilitation of the man who had been labelled "Number One Party Person in Power Taking the Capitalist Road" and "China's Khruschev" during the Cultural Revolution.

This turn of events, I realized very gradually over my months in China, was quite consistent with the new direction the leadership in China was taking. It represented the ascendancy of a set of principles that had been rejected throughout the years of the Cultural Revolution, and afterwards, during the rule of the Gang of Four. Liu Shaoqi had held that "in China, the revolution has been won," and that the main task ahead was the building of a sound, stable base for socialism. In order to build this economic base, he advocated a return to principles that had pulled China out of the very difficult years of the late Fifties, when famine and the withdrawal of Soviet aid had seriously jeopardized the gains of the revolution. These were principles of material incentives for workers, the encouragement of private plots and "free markets" for peasants, and the emulation of a Western (at that time, a Soviet) industrial model.

Mao, on the other hand, had not been so certain of the full victory of socialism in China, and he warned that vigilance was essential to safeguard the Party from the development of a bourgeoisie within its ranks. The entire Cultural Revolution has often been reduced to a "line struggle" between Mao and Liu, a struggle that Liu lost at the time. And indeed, I later heard from my students the theory that Mao had initiated the Cultural Revolution in order to defeat Liu.

Clearly, significant changes were taking place. Liu Shaoqi was one of the few remaining leaders toppled during the Cultural Revolution to have his name cleared, and, as I watched the Party Vice-Chairman, Deng Xiaoping, extend his belated condolences to Liu's widow, Wang Guangmei (herself recently released from prison), I puzzled over the implications of the memorial ceremony. The principles of limited encouragement of the profit motive that Liu had maintained were clearly in operation all around us, as Sichuan had been a sort of test province in the return to the "capitalist road" methods that Deng was advocating. Deng himself was formerly called "Number Two Party Person in Power Taking the Capitalist Road" and had twice weathered a fall from the leadership of China. Deng credits Mao for his second return to power in 1973, for it was Mao who summoned him back to Beijing to stand for re-election to the Party's Central Committee. Now Deng's "pragmatic" policies, very close to Liu's (except on the question of the emulation of the Soviet Union), define the current aims for China and the methods for reaching them.

In 1978, Deng reintroduced the "Four Modernizations" goal: he placed priority on developing and modernizing four key sectors of the Chinese economy — agriculture, industry, national defence, and science and technology — with the goal for China of reaching the status of a developed nation by the year 2000. This project entailed an entirely new "Westward-looking" approach, a reliance on American (notably not Soviet, as Liu Shaoqi had urged) input in the areas of technology and expertise.

When I arrived in China, my expectations of political signs were on the level of the dramatic activity we saw and heard reported during the Cultural Revolution. For example, I was surprised and somewhat disappointed that there were no longer any large, state-planned ceremonies on dates formerly celebrated, like May Day or May Fourth (the date in 1919 on which students erupted in nationalist demonstrations against the Versailles Treaty, which awarded German concessions in China to Japan). I had to learn to look at other events, other signs for indications of the direction China was taking.

The broader changes occurring in the country were apparent in many of the events we witnessed — the thriving "free markets" in the cities, where peasants sold the produce of their small private plots; the re-emergence of open religious activity we saw when we climbed Mt. E Mei; the municipal elections that took place in Chengdu in May; the university entrance examinations that the teachers of the province came to Sichuan University to mark; the broadening availability of films; the restoration of certain privileges, like our training course, to intellectuals; the importation of foreign technology, like the Japanese language lab about to be installed at Yunnan University; and the sometimes bitter, sometimes amused feelings we all shared in dealing with the bureaucratic hassles we encountered daily. In contrast to the practices that were allowed or encouraged in the past, these events, when taken as a whole, did indeed constitute a "rightward turn." Furthermore, the letters here show that there was general support for these changes among the people in my unit.

It struck me again and again while I was there that China is a country that changes very quickly, from month to month, yet is also a country that changes enormously slowly. We saw political facets of Chinese life — photo exhibits of Liu Shaoqi, for example, everywhere in Chengdu — that would not have been in evidence a couple of months before we arrived. But we also experienced political problems, such as grappling with the overwhelming power of the bureaucracy, that have been hallmarks of China for centuries. The indifference and elitism of officials is a subject attacked in Chinese editorials and political cartoons as a vestige of feudalism within the Party structure.

Exploring and commenting upon the levels of political change in China proved to be every bit as difficult as I had expected it to be, and it even took time for me to discover the complexity of the factors accounting for this difficulty. Soon after my arrival, I became aware of a debate over the relative economic merits of communism and capitalism, one that I certainly had not anticipated. This debate was represented to me by young people quoting with approval Deng Xiaoping's famous statement, "It doesn't matter if it's a white cat or a black cat, as long as it catches mice." The first obstacle I had to overcome in hearing remarks like this was my own surprise. I had expected that all debate on the political and economic future of China would presuppose the Maoist socialist framework; consequently, I found it almost shocking to hear remarks like "Mao Zedong Thought used to be our religion."

The depth of such criticism surprised me for another reason, as well. Before I left for China, I had learned that the other side of the new Dengist "pragmatic" policies was the removal of the "Four Great Freedoms" from the Chinese Constitution in early 1980. The "Four Freedoms" guaranteed Chinese citizens the right to speak out freely, to air views fully, to hold big debates and to put up wall posters (*dazibao*). Yet I detected little discernible concern at this apparently repressive move. Part of the explanation, I think, for my encountering so little reaction to the suspension of the Four Freedoms was the association with the Cultural Revolution, when political debate was a full-time activity. Also, it may be that the new economic freedoms which inspired so much support and enthusiasm balanced the loss of these political rights. And finally, people could simply have been unwilling to voice criticism of these moves in front of me. Yet, despite the removal of the Four Freedoms from the Constitution, open discussion of such fundamental questions as "communism or capitalism?" seemed encouraged rather than curtailed.

Another obstacle in my exploration of political questions was that the general discussion taking place was not truly accessible to me. My deficiency in the language was not the only factor preventing this access, because I was in daily contact with many people who spoke English. However, the conversations I did have were with intellectuals, a small segment of the population whose experiences during the Cultural Revolution often predisposed them to a distrust of the Maoist approach. Information about where the peasants stood on important issues, or the role that the People's Liberation Army might take in such debates, or the Party position, usually came to me second-hand, filtered through the attitudes of my university colleagues. Any Westerner in China experiences a degree of isolation from the mainstream of political debate because of the Chinese reluctance to open this arena to the scrutiny of foreigners. The tradition of judging contact with foreigners on a continuum ranging from problematic to suspicious is not simply a feature of the communist government. It is an outlook that long predates Liberation and is probably one result of the colonialist meddling in Chinese internal affairs in the nineteenth and twentieth centuries. In more recent times, during the Cultural Revolution, people generally avoided association with foreigners because of the strong insistence by the leadership that the creation of a proletarian culture was a task best taken on without the help of foreign influence.

It is also difficult to assess the internal effects of the tremendous changes in Chinese policies towards foreign powers since Mao's invitation to Nixon in 1972. However, China's alliance with the United States, fueled so directly by her fear of the Soviet Union, will be a crucial factor in the four areas targeted by the Modernization drive (agriculture, industry, defence and technology). The increasing Chinese awareness of the effects of this alliance on her internal organization and economic balance will entail continuing assessment of the risks of cooperating with such a power; it's therefore another area subject to great changes. Some of my students certainly disliked the influence of Western movies, music and clothing on Chinese youth. But they had difficulty, as I did, connecting these larger political alliances with any long-term effects on China's central institutions, like the commune system or the "iron rice bowl."

When I did manage to break through the cultural and political barriers to gain some insight into current political struggles, I had to remember that the stories and anecdotes I heard reflected attitudes that might not last very long. The attitude towards Mao is an example of this. While I was in China, the Party was preparing to embark on a massive re-evaluation of the Chairman's role before and after Liberation. A year later, the severe criticism of Mao that I had often heard became much less common with the publication of the Party's evaluation of him in June 1981. Mao was to be viewed, it stated, as a leader whose contribution to China was enormous, but he was also a leader who had indeed made mistakes — but not alone. This document criticized the entire Party for its own "leftism" in the years of the Cultural Revolution. Re-evaluations like these make it difficult for most observers in China to keep on top of the complex relationship between what is changing and what remains the same.

Quite typically, I think, for a Westerner, I was curious about the changes occurring among the young people of China and whether their opinions on marriage, sexuality and politics differed from those of the generations that had participated in the period of socialist building after 1949. I shared with some of my students their dismay at the consumeristic tendencies of the young people, but did not agree that this new development necessarily resulted from the Cultural Revolution. The argument I was offered was that the youth, disillusioned by their "wasted years" in the countryside and the betrayal of their loyalty to the leadership, were developing a scepticism that directed their values towards material goods. However, as I viewed the changes that were occurring — the reappearance of "movie stars" or advertising, for example — I had to conclude that the current policies toward consumerism seemed to be more directly involved in these new attitudes. And I frequently felt the irony of my situation: the affluent

Westerner, thoroughly experienced with the trap of consumerism, with its expensive advertising and wasteful packaging,
cannot really issue warnings against choosing that way of life. It
will be interesting to see if in the next few years those Chinese
now studying abroad will take up this task on their return.

Arriving in China as I did with a background as a socialist
feminist, I had long accepted something the women's movement brought to our political understanding in the West, that
"the personal is political," that there is no split between the
two spheres. In China, this connection has long been recognized, and the participation in the One Birth Movement is a
forceful example of a political choice intersecting a very
personal area of people's lives. This national policy, intended
to reduce overpopulation by restricting families to one, or at
most two, children, would probably be seen in the West as an
intolerable state intervention into our personal lives. Yet the
people we came into contact with accepted and supported this
policy, and they argued that a country as big, as poor and as
overpopulated as China had to take such firm measures.

Before I left for China, I was asked to get the "scoop" on the
position of women, the Gang of Four, the Cultural Revolution,
Mao, as well as the answer to the critical question, "Is China
turning away from socialist principles?" As I investigated and
reported on the developments going on around me in Chengdu
my letters continued to serve as "shock absorbers." But I
sometimes thought of my letters as strange newspapers that
appeared daily for my friends. Their headline stories were as
likely to be unimportant subjective commentary as events of
weighty political significance, like the memorial ceremony for
Liu Shaoqi. By piecing together the stories I heard and the
events I witnessed, I was hoping to carry out this assignment.

韓琳

The same ole place
Wednesday, July 9
Dear Carolyn,

The wonderful Sichuan food has begun to seem just a bit boring to us, and we are staggered by the amount of meat, mainly pork, that is put in front of us. We were asked, four or five weeks after we got here, what we would like to eat. When we said that we loved *doufu* (beancurd) and vegetables and (as diplomatically as possible) that we would like to have less meat, the leaders laughed politely, as if we had suggested eating warmed-up undershirts and stir-fried toilet paper. They explained that they prefer to give us lots of meat because that's special treatment. (So why ask for our preferences?) I think asking for *doufu* is like asking for peanut butter and jam sandwiches. More on food: watermelon season is just beginning, the peach season is in full swing, and pears are coming in, as are apples. We buy these in the "free markets" and then bring them back to our dining hall and put them in — this deserves a new paragraph —

Our New Refrigerator! This is the third fridge I've seen since being in China. There's one in the hotel bar that looks as if it was worn out before Liberation; the second one is in the apartment just below mine, belonging to the Japanese experts who are here for two years. They have *everything.* But ours (for all the experts to share) is a solid shining little Russian model, brand new, gleaming white on the inside, manufacturing ice cubes like a good comrade. It has fulfilled one of our deepest needs.

Of course I would be delighted to include the International Women's Day Committee on my lecture circuit when I return. I'm trying and trying to scoop lots of info on the Cultural Revolution and on women, but all I ever hear is that the lot of women is much better than before Liberation. Things on that level. What I'm really looking for is an "unreconstructed Maoist," but I've only read about them in the Western press. They must be in the hen's teeth category.

Ian jokingly told his class that he had come to China to find a wife. They went into shock. They could not *imagine* a Chinese marrying a foreigner! Ian offered to shave off his beard, learn Chinese and settle in China — yet even with all these obstacles removed, they said, no Chinese woman would have him. When they recovered, after multiple assurances that it was a joke, they soberly suggested that he had better settle for an overseas Chinese, or someone from Macao or Hong Kong...

DIARY ENTRY
Thursday, July 10

Hmmm, here's a slightly shocking bit of news noted in one of my student's diaries: "Two young robbers were executed because they robbed Chengdu Bank and killed a young woman who'd just taken a large sum of yuan out of the bank." This writer attributes the crime to the desire on the part of these two young men for "everything foreign" — I must say, the connection isn't perfectly clear to me.

DIARY ENTRY
Friday, July 11

One of my students had a very interesting entry from a newspaper in her diary today. It made me wonder whether I was reading new news, or old news, because I'd read a very similar story in Simone Leys' book, *Broken Images*. It has to do with the recent rehabilitation of Liu Shaoqi, the former president of China who died in prison. During the Cultural Revolution, he was branded the biggest "capitalist roader" of them all, and as my students put it, he was "persecuted to death."

The story my student reported on goes like this: at the beginning of the Cultural Revolution, when Liu Shaoqi was singled out for criticism, everyone correctly read the signs of the times and took down all their portraits of him and destroyed them. Anyone silly enough to keep a picture of Liu Shaoqi up would have been issuing a direct invitation to the Red Guards to come round. However, in some remote corner of China (my student doesn't say where), an old man harboured thoughts of rebellion and retained his admiration for Liu; so he did a very clever thing. He simply put a picture of Mao over the portrait of Liu, and put the framed picture back on the wall. And so it remained, covered by Mao all these years. Finally, this June, with the rehabilitation of Liu, this story came to light, and the original picture has been removed to some historical or revolutionary museum. And the old guy who did this is being congratulated for his loyalty and perspicacity through all these years.

Now, hunting up Leys' book, I find the following story. During the Cultural Revolution, one of Leys' informants, "T" explained that

> In his school, as everywhere else, there were giant bonfires of books from the library and from teachers' private libraries, as well as of books that had been confiscated in middle-class city homes. Stacks of books destined for the flames stood waiting in school court-yards. At night, T and a few comrades used to loot their school's pile of some dog-eared volumes that struck them as interesting, and would then swap their booty among themselves. He also described how the house of the great painter Liu Hai-su in Shanghai was sacked; the artist's own work and his collection were burned. One single painting was saved. It was hanging, under glass, in the living room, and the elderly artist had the presence of mind to cover it over with a large photograph of Mao.*

* Simone Leys, *Broken Images* (London: Alison and Busby, 1979), p. 110.

DIARY ENTRY
Thursday, July 17

The campus has emptied. All the students were leaving last weekend, carrying boxes strapped onto their backs, or satchels with a few enamel cups or tin food boxes tied onto their bundles, all off in groups of two or threes to catch a train or bus back to their hometowns for a six-week holiday. Some were going to be doing some serious travelling through China, up to Beijing or down to Guangzhou to see old schoolmates from middle school. Some were chuckling about the possibility of learning "new dances" and seeing more exciting things than are possible here in remote Sichuan.

Now an influx of teachers has taken over the campus — marking entrance exams for the university applicants under the strictest of security. With such a tiny ratio of university students to the entire population (one per cent), it is no wonder these exams take on such significance, and no wonder there's so much pressure on the kids who do make it into university. I'm not sure that I really approve of the reinstatement of these departmental entrance exams (which happened in 1977), but most people here see it as the reopening of tremendous possibilities. It concerns me that the general principle that was in operation before — the preference given to applicants of workers, peasant or soldier background — is no longer a priority.

I told one student, an undergraduate, that this reinstatement bothered me because it reminded me of the old Imperial Examinations and that China seemed to swing back and forth very dramatically on these kinds of policies.

"Oh, yes," he laughed. "But that's *very* Chinese."

DIARY ENTRY
Friday, July 18

Quite a rousing discussion on divorce in my class today. A great deal of concern was expressed over what would happen to the wife if the husband wanted a divorce and the wife didn't. (There was no concern about the wife initiating one, because the woman stands to lose a lot more in a divorce.) The new Marriage Law, enacted in 1950, allows for divorce if both parties want one; and only after complicated attempts at reconciliation have failed can a divorce be granted when only one party wants one. The position that less harsh divorce laws would be more humane was ridiculed: "Then people would get divorced three times a day!" But two of the students argued convincingly that a lot of harm had been done by the Chinese tradition of holding marriage so "sacred." And another student, who really has a lot of difficulty expressing himself, concurred: "Great harm was done by forced marriages in the past; many tragedies resulted from these people not being able to get divorces." My students were also shocked to discover the extent to which there are still arranged marriages in Japan today — they couldn't believe it possible in such a modern society.

韓琳

DIARY ENTRY
Saturday, July 19

Ah, it's happened — what we were nervous about has been resolved. Two days ago Miss Li delivered two straw mats for our beds, as she has been promising she would.

We were astonished at what they cost — 33 yuan ($22) each. Mary Ellen told me they were very cool to sleep on, so I dutifully scrubbed mine first, as instructed by Miss Li, hung it out to dry and tried it out on top of my padding. (Ian refused to have any part of his.) I didn't notice any difference — I still sweltered through the night.

DIARY ENTRY
Sunday, July 20

I have instituted a rule in class that I learned from Sharon — one that she applies much more extensively. I now collect five *fen* (3¢) from each person who speaks Chinese in class. Sharon is much stricter; she fines five *fen* per Chinese *word*! She also charges five *fen* each time a student draws a Chinese character. I find the habit of drawing a Chinese character, usually an imaginary one, in the air, or on the palm of your hand, or on your pantleg, sort of endearing, and I'm not so eager to see it eliminated. Sharon also doesn't allow spitting or littering in class, but I think it's more permissible for her to enforce those rules than for us to, because she's training scientists who are going abroad, people who need to know ahead of time what would be considered a *gaffe* in North America. It's interesting to discover what *we* do that repulses the Chinese — putting your fingers in your mouth for any reason is something that just isn't done; so that licking a finger to pick up a piece of paper or turn a page makes people wince, or turn away politely; and biting your nails, God forbid.

Another rule I've just instituted is having illuminating results, at least for me. I now allow my students to read the *Reference News*, the daily newspaper that they are eager to read, at break time *only* if they report on something from it. And from this, I become more informed — for instance, today I learned that some Chinese police will now be armed and able to shoot at criminals.

DIARY ENTRY
Thursday, July 24

A strange scene unfolded in my apartment tonight. Jiang, our interpreter, asked us the other day if he could bring some students from Chongqing to visit us. We agreed, but later found out that the leaders wanted to have a meeting with us tonight. We tried to reschedule the visit, but Jiang wouldn't hear of it. This was puzzling, as I would have thought the leaders' wishes would have taken precedence over the students', but we acquiesced.

Jiang arrived at exactly 7 p.m. and shocked Ian and me with the transformation in his demeanour: in a very teacherly, superior manner, he instructed the three students that "Now you will have free conversation."

What ensued was anything but. There were two young men and a young woman, who was afflicted with acute shyness and who did not say *one* word all evening, except "Thank you" when she left.

One young man had seated himself beside Ian and took out a crumpled page of notes and nervously consulted it from time to time as he poured out a speech on Canada. It was with amazement that we deduced, while he droned on for at least half an hour about Confederation in 1867 through to his latest information (which came up to the election of Joe Clark, but not the re-election of Trudeau; he was mortified when he discovered he didn't have the correct information on who our present Prime Minister is), that this must be a type of Chinese politeness. I remembered Miss Li panicking the night before she was to meet somebody from York University [in Toronto] on behalf of Sichuan University; she discovered with delight that Ian was a graduate of York, and so began to pump him for answers to questions like, "How many acres does York University have?" in order to present a decent "brief introduction" on York to this visitor *from* York.

Wednesday, July 30
Still here, more or less
Dear Penny,

Thanks for your letters. They're witty and sharp and we thoroughly enjoy them.

We hit the Jin Jiang Hotel for Jangled Foreigners with Sharon and her six-week female visitor, Sydney, the evening after we returned from E Mei, and found a *really* varied crew of foreign students there, from Togo, Japan, Nigeria, Sri Lanka and the Phillippines. The place had never seen anything like it; these students had a four-speaker tape recorder and plenty of disco and they just took over the place: turned off the lights, turned up their music, moved the tables and everyone got up to dance. The workers in the hotel, who are old hands at seeing weird Westerners (and Ian insists that people who tour in China are the weirdest-looking people in the world, and there's plenty of evidence to back him up) lined up behind the bar to watch the spectacle. One "girl" (all females are "girls" and males "boys" until married, at approximately 28) broke up laughing at the sight of us moving in the semi-darkness. The others simply stared. As usual.

Will you permit me a long protracted wail of, what? I was trying today to explain to Ian how I feel, and it's a combination of frustration, nervousness and utter impatience. You don't know how difficult life can be made here by the endless bureaucratic hassles and the stupid mistakes and assumptions that people are constantly making about us. This is much more negative than I've ever allowed myself to be, but this week I've had two too many of these experiences and twice I've burst out at the kind-hearted interpreter, Jiang and the "leaders." It's complicated, this story, but here goes.

The films. Finally, last week, 13 weeks after our initial request, the Canadian Embassy sent us a feature-length film, *J.A. Martin*. A technician kindly took care of picking it up while were off climbing Mt. E Mei. However, on our return, we found it couldn't be shown because — of all reasons! — it was locked in the technician's office, and he'd taken the keys with him to Chongqing. When I discovered that, I exploded in front of my class.

"This is the stupidest thing I have ever seen here! Do you know how long we've been waiting for that film? Do you know how many students and teachers in this department have asked us for a feature film? Do you know how much trouble the Embassy has given us? And now we have a movie, and we can't show it because it's locked in a room on the fifth floor!"

The students, shocked at my outburst (now here's something we've never seen before, they think) rallied somewhat, suggesting, "Break the door!" Even in my anger, I thought that was funny, but damned if I'd show it.

The leaders were tipped off that Maureen was upset, came and agreed that the situation was "stupid," and that, it seemed, was that.

But the plot sickens. The next day, one of Ian's students quietly passed him the word that the leaders were watching the film at that very moment (the projector being run by the vacationing technician, I suppose). Ah! The dawn of comprehension! Perhaps because of the film ban, the leaders felt they had to watch the movie before it was shown generally. But it infuriated me even further that I'd been given this ridiculous lie about it being locked up, when I would have understood perfectly that the leaders would want to check it out.

The outcome: finally, two days later, it was shown — to the entire university unit. And all our students thought it was boring.

The facilities in the department are very poor. The slide projector constantly snaps out of focus. The movie projector is a well-constructed sound scrambler that could be used by spies. Maybe it is. There are about 800 English books in the department library but they're incredible antiques and the good things (for example, *Jane Eyre*) are all "simplified versions" produced in Beijing. There's no language lab, though all the classrooms are wired for individual tape recorder use — but that set-up is used for listening classes, not ours. Frequent power cuts (at least once weekly) have to be planned around, so we have to bring batteries for our taped lessons on no-juice days...

Okay, you get the picture, you deserve some good news after wading through all that groaning. There was Mary Ellen's wonderful visit, and the spectacular climb up Mt. E Mei, when we got to be very good friends with Cheng Qilong, our student and Chinese teacher. And there's our new friendship with Sydney and Sharon. And of course work continues: we're starting to teach a new class one afternoon a week, people going abroad who want to learn "living words"...

DIARY ENTRY
Thursday, July 31

I had Cheng Qilong, who is now our Chinese teacher, translate a poem in one of the tourist books I bought:

> Lying on a big rock
> with a harp
> watching a white crane fly away,
> waiting for the clouds to come back.

But I forgot to ask him the poet's name. Dumb.

Monday, August 4
Hot old Chengdu
Dear Janet,

Well, the first thing you must do as soon as you finish reading this letter is to get in touch with Penny to tell her that I am (finally) restored to my usual high spirits. I wrote her a letter last week and told her in vivid detail of just one hassle that we've been going through (over getting our films shown). I got so incredibly impatient with the incidents of incompetence and unconcern that I blew my stack. It's all a result of frustration and impatience: one is reduced, even if one has the language, to being totally dependent on others because certain facilities just don't exist. In order to get permission to go to Xian for a weekend, one just can't phone up and reserve a flight. No. First, feel the situation out with the interpreters, ask them to do some of the spadework (which they forget about), then request a meeting with the Foreign Affairs office of our university, then *have* the meeting, then get permission from your "unit" (like getting permission from your boss to go to New York for a weekend), then arrange the flight for selves and interpreter, getting as much of a hand in the arrangements as possible so they don't book you to the wrong city.

Okay, okay, my superego is screaming; my sense of perspective is all unbalanced and frayed on account of these knots. I know the outlook I should have, but, I'm sorry, I've temporarily mislaid it amidst the impatience and shock of losing our customary autonomy. So I lose sight of the value of the unit. For your historical edification: in the old days, you had next to no mobility unless you were attached to a rich, well-placed family. Now everybody's got a unit, and so, cumbersome and peculiar and interfering as all these levels of permission appear to us, things ultimately do get finalized — like, for example, our long-awaited trip to Mount E Mei which we returned from last week.

Anyway, the mountain was a *killer*. We had pooh-poohed all the students' warnings about how hard it would be, and Ian had kept announcing to his class that he was going to the top. First of all, it was blisteringly hot, with cicadas screaming as if they were being electrocuted to death all over the place. Secondly, the climbing is a matter of flight after flight after flight after flight of endless steep jagged stone steps set at terrifying angles to each other and the cliffs they overlook. It often rains quite heavily in the night and the early morning, so that by mid-morning the steps are covered with a juicy layer of red clay mud. This doesn't affect the climbing much, but oh! the descending. Both Ian and I discovered the meanings of words that were quite common in our vocabulary before: "arduous" and "treacherous." Thirdly, this is summer vacation, so the mountain is *crowded*, with hundreds of students climbing for their vacations. They would nimbly pass us (we got winded after one flight and never quite recovered, though we kept climbing), the ones from more affluent families proudly sporting their tape recorders.

But what made the experience really remarkable instead of five days of torture (which it essentially was) was seeing the revival of Buddhism in China. It's said that if you climb to the top, you will never die. Well, there were all these old ladies doing just that. They were all at least 70, about 4'6", gnarled and bent over, wearing the old lady uniform (those jackets that do up with frogs at the side, near the armpit; always in blue) and straw sandals with bits of corn husk between the toes to keep the sandals from rubbing. Such determination! One of Ian's students explained to me, "They're just as tired as we are, but they never stop to rest, and the first thing they do when they arrive at the temples is to pray to the Buddha, prostrating themselves." These old ladies would come up behind us, saying "*Man zou*: Take care, go slowly; the Buddha goes with you," pick their way past us, arrive way ahead of us at each temple, and then shout with glee when they saw us coming, red-faced, out of breath and cranky, and say, "You're so young and energetic." Hah! We felt like the biggest tubs of flab the Western world ever imposed on the East. I got several pictures of men carrying these old women, some with formerly bound feet, down the mountain in baskets on their backs. Most of them, if they were carried, were carried *down* the mountain because it's so dangerous. One man from Sharon's university was killed last year when he was taking a picture (stepped backwards off a cliff, eeks) and while we were on the mountain, a little boy was carried down because he'd fallen and gotten a head wound.

It was a nice break, though. And we did some of the climbing with our students. We broke a few Chinese rules and invited some of our students to sleep in the extra beds in our rooms because the Chinese quarters were so crowded (sometimes three or four to a double bed!). We all kept *that* a secret.

An interesting cultural conflict — interesting because it was such a strong one — was how most of the younger Chinese handled this devoutly religious scene. They would laugh and mock, pretend to "kow-tow" (which is originally a Chinese word for prostrating to the Buddha and means "knock head on floor") and make fun of the incense and offerings put in front of the statues. I had never realized how ingrained it is in us not to make fun of people's religious beliefs, and I had to restrain my fury. And I suppose I'm a person who sides with the "opiate of the people" line on religion. In fact, this "opiate" viewpoint was probably strengthened on Mount E Mei; I think that the more grinding their poverty, the more people turn to religion. The majority of these old women were certainly poor. (Those who had bound feet would not have come from a poor peasant background —

having bound feet was a sign your family didn't need your labour.)

Just to complete the picture — the scenery was spectacular. One could finally understand Chinese art, seeing the bamboo-lined paths, the rushing waterfalls down craggy rocks, the suspended bridge in the distance, the temple at the top of the mountain. And oh, I saw a monkey!

We climbed up for two days and down for one and a half; we didn't make it to the top (which annoyed some of the little old ladies) although our students went on ahead. They were rewarded with the E Mei experience: seeing the sunrise, the "sea of clouds" (mountain peaks above the clouds) and the "Buddha lights." In the late afternoons, when weather conditions are right, red circular rings of light, sort of like small rainbows, appear in the air just below the mountain-top. The inexplicable thing about the "Buddha lights" is that you can wave your hand at the same time as another person many feet away, but each person sees only his or her own shadow. They were lucky the weather was good enough to see all this: many people do make it to the top, but have rainy, cloudy weather. If we'd had two more days, Ian and I would have made it. But as it is, I suppose we shall die. I thought I was going to die then and there, of aching thigh and calf muscles.

The experience when I got home was one in a chain of things that set off my enraged letter to Penny: when I got up the three flights to my place, fantasizing about a hot bath in which to soak my aching filthy limbs, I found that somebody had locked my inner doors (to each room) and gone off with the keys. The water was also turned off that day. Ian proposed that he fling himself down on his bed to have a good cry, get it over with, and then vacate his bed so that I could fling myself down on it.

Ah, another late night — me, the only one typ the darkness.

DIARY ENTRY
Wednesday, August 6

Today one of the students gave an oral report that created quite an uproar. The report itself went along smoothly, but when the rest of the class got a chance to ask questions, all hell broke loose.

The report concerned the time this student had spent in the countryside during the Cultural Revolution. He had been assigned to work in a mill in the mountains. When production in the mill was shut down in order to allow the workers to engage in political study and activity, he stated that many of the mill workers went up the mountainside and cut down choice trees, carted them home and busied themselves making sets of furniture. Essentially this was an accusation of theft: the trees belonged to the state, and weren't there for the taking. But he reported this blandly, among a lot of other details. He said that, in time, the leaders put an end to this practice, especially as the workers often chopped down an entire tree, cut away the best part, and left the rest of the tree to rot on the mountainside.

The rest of the students were horrified and outraged. They demanded to know if the student giving the report had taken part in any of this stealing of lumber and production time. Yes, the student admitted, but he had made only a box for his few possessions, while others had made whole sets of furniture for their homes. Again they were aghast; one student, a Party member, was much less upset than the others, and seemed to be aware of such incidents, whereas the majority of the class were shocked to learn of these goings-on.

"That was a very common practice in those times," explained the Party member. "And it was very badly handled by the Party. The leaders did nothing about such things for a very long time, and because they did nothing, some people simple continued doing it. It's not correct to blame them; it was the Party leaders who didn't put an end to that kind of self-interest who were responsible."

People didn't seem to be much assuaged by this comment, and continued barraging the poor student with questions. I've never seen a reaction quite like this one; I would have expected cynicism, but not outrage.

DIARY ENTRY
Thursday, August 7
Xian

Our early-morning flight landed the three of us, Ian, his student Deng Ying (our interpreter for the trip) and me in Xian about one o'clock, which was a little late to arrange sightseeing for the day, so we spent the afternoon shopping.

It was a shock for Deng Ying to find out the kinds of things I liked. In the antique section of the Friendship Store, I found some silver hairpins that I was enchanted with. Deng Ying shook her head.

"Those are awful," she said.

"Oh, I like them," I said. "In fact, I think they're beautiful."

"But they're for old ladies. Old ladies don't even wear them anymore," she commented, shaking her head again and continuing. "They're the kind of things that, if we found them, we would throw in the garbage. Actually my grandmother did have some, and when she died, we threw them out. I can't believe anybody is trying to sell them."

"Well," I answered lamely, "I like old things. Hand-made things. Lots of people back home would like these."

"I can't understand it. They are by no means beautiful," she said with grim finality.

DIARY ENTRY
Saturday, August 9
Xian

The China Travel Service guide who met us at the airport has had a complete change of heart. On Thursday, in her cool-as-a-cucumber manner, she announced that it would cost us 200 yuan ($135) for the use of a car for three days and that we could not get anywhere without one. "Absolutely out of the question," said Ian. "That's an entire month's salary." And we proceeded to negotiate for the price of the car for one afternoon only, to get us to the tomb of Qin Shih Huang. She was astounded that we intended to take the bus or walk to the other tourist sights — or she feigned astonishment, I don't know which. Deng Ying said that she would do exactly the same as the guide: "She's trying to make as much money as she can for her unit." Aaah, I see.

Today we went to Banpo Village, an archeological site that was discovered in the 1950s and is over 6000 years old. The thing that fascinated me most about it was that the society of the village was matriarchal. I asked Ian and Deng Ying to imagine what a present-day matriarchal society would be like. When Deng Ying realized that I was honestly questioning whether she could see China run by women, with a Central Committee of 200 women and a handful of men, she became serious. And what she had to say really shocked me: she maintained that women are not capable either of equality or of running a nation as big and as important as China.

"But what do you mean, not capable? How do you know?" She replied that women are just not as intelligent as men, that this was a simple fact.

"How do you know women aren't as intelligent as men? How can you say that?" I pushed.

"I know it from my experience as a teacher; we see it all the time. Young girls, when they graduate from middle school, may be as intelligent as the boys, but when they get to university, the boys always surpass them."

"Does that really happen? Why do you think that?"

"It's true," she maintained. "Women aren't as strong as men physically, and they're not as smart, intellectually. It's just biology."

"Well, I don't believe that," I said, and went on to explain that I thought that, for so long, women's opportunities have been so narrow and so circumscribed by social realities that it wasn't fair to judge what we were capable of on the basis of what we had accomplished in the past. And then, feeling that my arguments were not having much effect, I said, "You know, this whole question of women is something that I have done a lot of work on back home. And the example of women in China has always been very important to us in North America. All the ballets and slogans of the Cultural Revolution —"

"I know, I know, 'Women hold up half the sky,' " she interrupted.

"Yes, that slogan is very well-known in North America; it's been very influential in the women's movement there," I said. "And I still think it's a good slogan, even if it isn't popular here any more."

"Yes, yes, it *is* true, you're right," she agreed. "In fact," she added, lapsing into incorrect English, "even some women can hold up one hundred per cent of the sky!"

Then and there, I decided it would be a good idea to give a talk on women and the women's movement in North America . . .

We visited the Bell Tower in the centre of the city — and I was surprised to find that it wasn't open to the Chinese, only to foreigners. Then, back to our hotel, and as we approached the big empty square that characterizes the centre of Chinese cities (and always seem to me to be ringing with the ghost voices of Red Guards), what had been slow steady rain changed into a bucketing, drenching downpour; it was raining so heavily that we had trouble keeping our balance as we ran. The three of us started laughing giddily as we zigzagged across the square, and Deng Ying said it was raining alcohol, because it was making her weave so much. Then, as we turned, panting and laughing, into the hotel grounds, she hesitated before she said to me,

"Push your hair back off your face so you don't look like such a foreign devil."

"What?" cried Ian. "Did you call Maureen a foreign devil? You do still call us 'foreign devils'!"

"No, no, no," she protested, "It's just that, with your hair falling all over your face like that, you look just like a picture of a foreign devil."

We collapsed in the hotel, had dinner and paid our food bill in shock at the reduction in prices that Deng Ying had been able to accomplish, although her food prices for her own meals were even lower. She maintained it was all because "people respect college teachers very much."

This vacation has made me very self-conscious about spending and consuming, although I realize that is the opposite effect that the Chinese would like to see. It has been an eye-opener experiencing the tourists' China: we have straggled up to sites and towers and temples very much on our own, either walking there or taking a public bus, but at each place we are encountered by busloads of tourists disgorging at theatre events, factories, schools just ahead of us. People swarm in, visit the site, then go to the shops attached and sit around in the *waibin* waiting room having tea, and then leave. I always thought that we had very little contact, being isolated at the university, but compared to the tourists, we are practically living in the pockets of the Chinese! And I never understood, till now, why the tourists' schedule is so exhausting — what appears to be an attempt to control the tourists' movements is really an effort to bring more money in, to spread valuable foreign currency to as many units as possible.

DIARY ENTRY
Wednesday, August 13

Susan gave her oral report in class today; it was on "The standards of Choosing Husbands and Wives in Chengdu." She's one of the people who has been taking very seriously her "responsibility" to learn and teach about the contrasts in our two cultures. She was also the one who wanted me to explain a hotdog and a hamburger; this sent me searching through the pile of magazines we brought with us and keep in our office for reference and lending. I was, at the same time, looking for a picture of a kitchen chair like the one mentioned in the story we were studying, "Benny" by Mordecai Richler. So I picked up a *Family Circle*, explaining that it was essentially a "women's magazine." That remark made her suggest to one of the male students looking on as we leafed through the magazine that he shouldn't be looking. I pooh-poohed the suggestion, and then we ran smack-dab into an ad for Modess maxi-pads, which I was asked to explain. When the male student caught on (after the second explanation, as did the three women who were also there), he backed out the office door in embarrassment.

The gist of her talk was that a deplorable change was taking place among the young people of China, but it had not yet been transmitted to the young people of Chengdu. This was the tendency of young men to look for women who were beautiful, rather than "tender," and of young women to seek future husbands who could offer material comforts, like "the three runnings" (a watch, a sewing machine, and a bicycle), rather than husbands who were "kind-hearted" or who had "political integrity." An illuminating, heated and hilarious discussion ensued. The men, most of them married, were convinced that the young women of Chengdu were also afflicted with this new trend to place a man's ability to provide above personal qualities and political soundness. There was a lot of laughter, but I sensed a real bitterness beneath it, because some of the men pointed out that a teacher, especially an English teacher, is not a real "catch" despite the (returning) honour of his position; the reason he wouldn't be such a catch is that his salary as a beginning teacher at 48 yuan a month is even lower than a worker's, at about 60 yuan. I noticed that the two or three men who aren't married sat quietly through the discussion, looking a little pained and offering no comments as the others disputed hotly and joked.

"Haven't you heard of the ten advantages that every young man must have in order to get married?" demanded one man of Susan.

"Yes, I have, but I bet you couldn't name them if you tried," she challenged back.

"Oh, I know them," he said somewhat sorrowfully, and began to name them. "The first one is the three runnings..."

"No, no, no!" laughed some of the other men. "You've got them all wrong!"

"All right, what are they? Do you know?" said the student to Garry (another student who had wanted an English name).

Garry had them down perfectly, and recited: "The first is a set of furniture; the second is no parents; the *third* is the three runnings; the fourth is four seasons of clothing for the woman; the fifth is that he is handsome; the sixth is that he is not concerned with other relatives; the seventh is that his salary is over 70 yuan a month; the eighth is that he is capable in social intercourse; the ninth is that he neither drink nor smoke; and the tenth is that he must be obedient."

"Wait, wait, wait," I intervened, scribbling madly to get them all down. "I've heard of the 'three runnings' before, but where in the world did these 'ten advantages' come from?"

"Oh, it's just a joke," some of the students explained.

"Well, I know it's not serious," I answered, "but where did this come from? You all seem to know them."

"Oh, it's a popular 'crosstalk,' " one student answered. A crosstalk is the English word that is used to describe a Chinese comedy routine between two people, always men.

"This number eight, 'capable in social intercourse' — does that mean being good at using the 'back door'?"

"Yes, that's right, that's right," everybody laughed.

"And what about number two, 'no parents'? Does that mean that the man shouldn't have to take care of elderly parents?" I asked.

"Yes," everyone answered.

"But that's awful!" I gave a look of disapproval.

"Oh, well, at least he should have *young* parents, so that he doesn't have to take care of them right away," someone amended.

"But really," I tried to make the conversation more serious, "do young women look for these things?"

"Absolutely not," the young women, a small band of four, asserted strongly.

"Yes, they do, they do," the men tried to counter the women.

Susan reasserted control over the discussion. "Some girls are like that," she said, "but not all. In big cities, like Shanghai and Beijing, the girls are getting more and more like that, but not so much here." She was returning to her original point.

"Oh, that's not true! It's everywhere in China!"

"Well, okay," I said. "Let's say it's *starting* to happen, that young people are getting more consumeristic, and that you don't like this change."

"Right," everyone agreed.

"But what do you think is the cause of it? Why is it starting to happen now?" I asked.

To my frustration, everyone drew blank looks, and no one could offer an explanation for the development of these new values.

韓珠

August 14
Chengdu
Dear Michael,

I thought it might be a nice idea to write you from your old "bedroom," somewhat reassembled, so you can get the flavour of Chengdu again. Your letters caused all the excitement you anticipated and it was with a certain amount of chagrin that we heard they still have croissants in Paris.

The negotiations about Lhasa have been, and still are, interminable and tedious, but the magic solution to all the obstacles was our offering to pay for the trip ourselves. It's going to cost a bundle, even if we get the foreign experts' rates on flight (600 yuan) and hotel (150 yuan per night). Outrageous. No wonder the unit was throwing around all these obstacles, like saying we needed permission from the Central Committee! We'll send you a postcard if we get there.

Our last month here is shaping up exactly like our first. For a while there in the middle, there was a lull, and people began to take us mercifully for granted. We actually had a few evenings or afternoons a week free, and visits or trips weren't scheduled for our Sundays. We didn't know whether to be relieved or resentful. But it was peaceful, and we finally began to feel rested. However, now that we have only three more weeks here, a panic has set in, and there's a flood of requests for taping, scripting, lectures, extra classes and groups — all of which we have foolishly agreed to. You'll remember this scene.

The heat is over. Someone abruptly turned it off one morning this week and our students, all wearing jackets again, announced it was now fall. None of this gentle sliding into seasons, although one student said that there were a few "fall tigers" yet to come.

Now, let's see. Changes. Also this week, with exactly the same kind of abruptness, the old printing house at the end of the block on the way to the dining hall was torn down. Why? They are going to build, get this, a three-storey recreation centre for experts — it will include a restaurant, a dance floor, a small store, a billiards room and God-knows-what else. I suggested a delicatessen and a dry cleaner's. This is in addition to the *two* residences now near completion. We've heard that they're expecting to have 50 or 60 experts by 1985. Ah, the benefits accruing to a "key university."

Another change is that we've made a new friend whom I'm sorry you never got a chance to meet — an American woman at Chengdu University of Science and Technology. Sharon Hare is terrific. She has had us over for dinner as well as lectures, plays, mock conferences and of course we have had several drink-ups at the Jin Jiang. I don't want you to get the wrong impression of her; she's also been given a Model Worker award by her university.

Now, things remaining the same. Everything, essentially. The Café Vienna has become a favourite haunt of the *waiguo ren* express, as we call it (Lex Deux Magots didn't sustain its initial momentum). The caretakers in our building are still evilly influenced by the Cultural Revolution. Miss Li is her same old self. Ian's toilet still doesn't work, although the workers come to look at it every week. I still get off my bike The Chinese Way and on The Stupid Way, although it was a bit difficult to maintain doing it The Chinese Way when I was wearing a skirt. The Jin Jiang River is still polluted. We still have coughs. We are still plagued in the streets by people wanting grammar explanations.

Now you have to hear about our accomplishments. You would not be impressed with our pronunciation, but you would be proud of our progress in Chinese. We can handle money transactions, bargain hesitantly, tell people where we're going, inform Comrade Li when we're not going to be there for meals, ask the caretakers for sheets, have our bike tires filled with air, and get some things to eat, including ice cream at the Café Vienna. Which is delicious, by the way. We can now buy Goldfish toilet paper and mosquito coils without Miss Li's assistance. Just as I'm beginning to understand and be understood, we're leaving.

Accomplishment #2 is finding a Source for the Kunming coffee you used to rave about, those wonderful black aromatic molecules from the Vietnamese coffee shop; a connected accomplishment is rigging up something to make it in. Another accomplishment is climbing Mount E Mei, though not to the *Jing Ding* (Golden Summit). That is a very long story. Another time. Something I am very proud of is the fact that we learned how to make *jiaozi* this week.

I suppose one accomplishment that we all have to share is the fact that some of our students now, in their writing and speaking, sound fairly natural, much less as if they stepped out of the pages of a Bronte novel that has been rewritten by the folks at the *Beijing Review*. It's really been a joy, and I only wish I could start another five-month session all over again. I'd know where to begin this time. Maybe. There's an incredibly nice feeling in our classrooms, and it's going to be wrenching to leave the students. Ech, I won't think about that right now.

I must get to bed. We're going to the Dujiangyan irrigation system tomorrow morning at 7:30, and I hear that there is a mountain nearby that we have to climb. Shades of E Mei, groan.

DIARY ENTRY
Friday, August 15

We're all conscious in class of how time is running out, and the students are madly copying out by hand whole books that we brought with us. The conflict over the content and style of our teaching, which went subterranean for a while, has surfaced again. What *I* would prefer to do is to begin to work intensively on methodology and give them tips, techniques and teacher training. However, what *some* students would like is for us to teach idioms — "in the red," "below the belt," "put your foot in your mouth" — instead.

The water has been off for 48 hours and I'm in desperate need of a bath; I managed to deal with my hair today by having it washed in the hairdresser's at the hotel. Ah, the pleasure of having warm water on one's scalp — the second time this summer. Ian got his hair cut, hilariously short. I think the barber working on him this time, unlike the experienced one Miss Li took him to before, was frightened by — eeks! — curly hair, and simply tried to do it the fastest way; he didn't use the scissors but just passed clippers all over his head. Now Ian's ears are astonishingly apparent; I keep chuckling when I ride behind him on the bike.

Tonight we gave the last in our series of banquets for our students. This one was for the students who come from Chengdu, and I must say they chose an excellent restaurant: The Happiness and Glory Garden, which, we were informed, was founded in 1911 and has a branch in

New York. Everyone was in a sparkling mood, and one of Ian's students was celebrating his birthday (so we sang) and he announced that his hobby was drinking beer. Both of these things are very non-Chinese. Miss Li had just finished saying, "Not me," to my suggestion that everybody was a bit drunk when she stood up, reached out and grabbed the soup tureen and cried, "Bottoms up!" But the really warm note came from the student in Ian's class who told us to call him "Run-Away" because that's what his name sounds like. "What shall we toast to?" we asked. "To *pengyou*-ship!" he suggested, coining a word that's half Chinese and half English and that means "friendship."

We had fabulous food as well — 15 dishes in all: a Chengdu specialty of hot chicken with the wonderful "numbing" spice called *huajiao*, pork, goose, duck, roasted soy beans (especially for me, as I'm allergic to peanuts), an excellent meatball dish, a splendid deep-fried chicken dish with sweet sauce that was my favourite, and two excellent soups to end the meal: a sweet one, made from plums, and a "salt" one. We drank beer and ate rice throughout the meal as has been our custom at all these banquets — a departure from Chinese custom that is now accepted with equanimity.

Deng Ying noted that the cost of the meal, 60 yuan (about $40), was precisely the amount that Ian is selling her his bicycle for. "We've just eaten up the bicycle, if you know what I mean!" she said.

DIARY ENTRY
Saturday, August 16

Today Miss Li took us shopping — cleavers and woks and steamers that I want to take home. Then she and her husband took us to a restaurant which is the original home of *MaPou Doufu,* a wonderful Chengdu dish with beancurd in a hot, soupy sauce that is spiced with the Chengdu "flower spice," *huajiao.* I have an insatiable passion for this dish, and so I also bought a lot of these spices to take home.

When we got home at four, I was horrified to discover two rats, each caught in their rat-traps that Jiang had bought for us. I got the poor, unsuspecting leader who was giving us the banquet tonight to pick them up and carry them out — I just couldn't face it, and blanched when he held them up to show me how big they were. That delayed our leaving for the restaurant with his family. And then, on our way, I did another spectacularly inappropriate thing: I rode into him, and nearly knocked us both off our bikes! (I was craning my neck to look at Sharon's teaching building as we rode through her university.) Ian was in stitches.

The banquet was excellent, though we had had so many fine meals in the past 24 hours that it was a bit lost on us. We started talking about the Cultural Revolution, of course, and specifically I was curious about the rivalry between our university and the one next to it, where Sharon teaches. I got a glimpse of what people mean when they talk about the difficulties created within families during that time, because the leader and his wife were on different sides, "separated in opinion": she supported the students of the next university, who were aligned with the Chongqing students; he supported the students of our university. They said there was heavy fighting, with guns, between the two universities in 1967 and 1968. Our university lost ten or 12 students and about six or eight from the next university were killed. This was in addition to the blaring loudspeakers that each university had trained on the other through the nights.

DIARY ENTRY
Sunday, August 17

A surprise visitor tonight: our Canadian expert friends in Guangzhou have a student who comes from Chengdu; so, home on his holidays, he looked us up and brought greetings from the Canadians. He was like a breath of fresh air, different from so many of our visitors who want to have texts explained — he wanted to chat, and about politics, my favourite subject. I was taken aback by how critical he is of China: "Mao was Marxist, The Gang was Marxist, Deng is Marxist — who is the real Marxist?"

We also heard some juicy bits of gossip from him. One was that a *dazibao* (a big-character poster) was put up this year at the Guangzhou Foreign Language Institute, protesting the fact that students weren't getting a chance to be taught by foreigners; this occurred in spite of the fact that *dazibao* are no longer legal, another thing he complained about. He also complained about the banning of the "democratic wall" in Beijing. He told us something that we hadn't heard about here, too: that a magazine called *Jin Jiang*, put out by the students of the Chinese Department at Sichuan University, was suspended this year for its criticism of the Cultural Revolution and its accounts of the "bitter experiences" people in Sichuan had during that period. This puzzled me; I thought free ventilation of the bitterness and criticism of the Cultural Revolution was officially permitted, but perhaps these students went too far — and criticized Mao. Although criticism and very sharp words about Mao are something we hear a lot, I don't think this is officially condoned.

It is difficult to know how to interpret all this. A lot of what this student said was disjointed, and both Ian and I wondered if he might have been simply repeating what he'd heard foreigners say, following the time-honoured Chinese tradition of stating what the respected listener wants to hear. For example, he spoke of Chinese foreign policy, and said it was very strange that the leaders were adopting a course of friendship with capitalist countries like the United States, and with fascist countries like Chile. I've never heard any Chinese grumble about China cosying up to the U.S., let along be critical of Chinese ties with Chile. I also wondered if studying in Guangzhou, so close to Hong Kong, made him more open to the whole Hong Kong consciousness. Who knows?

August 17, eeks
Dear Abby,

Greetings from the (or *a*) land of public ownership. Many many thanks for the quick response to the SOS for the words to that Canadian classic, "The Frozen Logger." But now the students have decided that they don't want to put on an English evening, which, frankly, is just as well — an enormous amount of work has been circumvented. The students were relieved when we said okay to their counter-proposal of just having a party for ourselves. Personally, it annoyed me a little because *I* was quite willing to get up onstage and make a gigantic fool of myself by singing a song or two in Chinese to an audience of Chinese people who would have been there mainly to see me and Ian. Oh, well.

China is really a very special place, and I think the thing that tantalizes me is that I know I could live a lifetime here and still be learning about it. I feel like we're leaving before we get started and so my mind keeps supplying this "next time I'll come for two years" thought. And then I fantasize about how I would do things differently, and assure lots more contact with people. One of the things that makes me feel this way is that I was in the deepest of culture/language shock for the first two months and could barely learn a word of Chinese.

It's going to be terrible to leave the students. They're such a funny mix of characteristics — critical and very forthright ("That was a very good lesson," "Why don't you wear nicer shoes?"). But the women are openly affectionate with me, and say things like "I feel very shy about telling you this, but from the bottom of my heart I feel so grateful to have had you for a teacher." They are forever admiring our dedication, which is proven by things like coming to class even though it's raining (not hard, either). It seems as if people appreciate the wrong things, but appreciate them deeply. I suppose that's what cultural differences are all about.

Politically, things are quite discouraging, at least from my standpoint. I told you about Mao being personally blamed for the problems of the Cultural Revolution. Here's a quote from one student's diary, for example:

> In China, the Great Cultural Revolution was the worst disaster-ridden war, both on the land and in people's minds. It was without parallel in history. This is not to mention that it held back the economic development of the whole country. The deaths of thousands of people, the breaking up of countless families and the destruction of property will forever make history itself feel pain.
> And why did Mao Zedong launch such a terrible war? The people and history will soon answer.

There are other heavy things, like the incredible bureaucracy. And then there are all the galling privileges that Party cadre have in comparison to ordinary folks, and the crisis of faith in the Party that is a consequence of all this privilege. This lack of faith and respect is fairly open, although there still remains some "timidity" in confronting the abuses left over from the days of the Cultural Revolution, or so I'm told. And then there are the long-standing problems caused by feudalism. Like attitudes towards women. Two of our eight women students have quite frankly told me that men are superior to women, especially intellectually. The men are not interested in discussing it, but will give you lots of fine-

sounding talk about how women have "stood up" since
Liberation. Well, I suppose they have; but out of 200 in
the Central Committee I'm told there are only about 15
women. This is *with* a quota. More men do help out at
home, though.

Do you know that I've *counted* the pregnant women
I've seen since I arrived in China, and that the total is six!
There were probably more at that party you went to.

Great big 16-ounce wine glasses full of Xs and Os.

Monday, August 18
Dear Betty and Colm,

Last week Ian and I did two presentations on religion to
our classes — he on Judaism (for some reason, they
thought he was just "pretending" to be Jewish!) and I on
Catholicism. The Irish question came up, so I volunteered
to show my slides. Which I did, of course. Weird to be
showing Dingle and Dublin and Donegal in the middle of
southwest China, plus a lightning-quick history of
Ireland.

I was quite pleased with my slide show on Ireland — I
presented the country in terms of "stereotypes" (poets,
large families, drinking, politics, religion, music, friendliness and of course the *green* of it all) mostly in order to
attack the notion of stereotypes. As entertaining as the
show was, I think the concept of stereotyping was lost on
them.

Ian just came in and brought with him two bundles of
magazines that a friend had mailed from home. Among
them was a *Cosmopolitan*, a *People* plus the usual sober
stuff — *Maclean's*, *The Economist*, etc. This is the first
time in months I've seen trash like *Cosmo* and *People*,
and I had a glimmer of what re-entry shock is going to be
like. I can't help looking at articles like "Why American

Women (Still) Don't Get What They Want in Bed"
through Chinese eyes — which is not to say that I really
have an idea of what the Chinese think of it all. I'm sure
I'll find out; our students are hungry for Western
magazines. But it's funny, they don't notice the pictures
so much, but they devour the copy in ads. You can't
imagine how difficult it is to explain some of that copy.
One student had Ian go over, line by line, a Vic Tanny's
ad ("I dropped eight inches off my waist..."). And a
student of mine thought a kitchen ad was a laboratory. I
can see why. It looked so hygienic, with all those
gleaming instruments, and a lone woman smiling in the
middle of that space. People are really short on space
here. It looked very scientific. And spotless.

DIARY ENTRY
Tuesday, August 19

It seems that when my students decide to give their oral
reports on something related to the Cultural Revolution,
a heavy reaction can be guaranteed. The student who
spoke today explained that he had chosen his topic — a
battle that occurred in his home county in Sichuan —
because today was the thirteenth anniversary of that
event.

He began with a history of the Cultural Revolution,
which was mostly for my benefit, I suppose, because I'm
sure everyone else was familiar with the chronology. The
Cultural Revolution was launched in 1966 by Mao, and in
January of 1967, the people of Shanghai wrested power
away from the "capitalist roaders" in the Party by seizing
control of the newspapers, factories and municipal
government. At that time, two factions prepared to seize
local political power in his home county: the "rebel"
group made up of students and intellectuals was called

Dongfang Hong (the East is Red); and the other group was made up of the peasants, and though weaker in arguing and pushing their line, they were actually stronger in numbers. Despite police intervention in February, the peasant grouping managed to gain three bases in his town: the theatre, the hospital and the primary school. For the next six months, the two factions secretly armed themselves, and finally battles to "liberate" sections of the county took place.

There are other analyses, of course, of the line divisions: one is that the sons and daughters of the Party cadres — whether of worker, peasant or soldier background — formed the "loyalist" factions. The opposing factions, the "rebels," were not the children of leaders, and they reversed Mao's statement on the Party: "95% of the cadre are good and 5% are bad." They argued that only 5% were good. This wasn't the analysis my student gave, by the way.

On August 19, 1967, the fighting in his home town lasted all day and into the night. He mentioned, with a smile, the tank that one of the groups had fashioned out of a tractor, a crude-looking affair that actually succeeded in making the other group think it was well-armed. But his manner got a little grimmer as he described the shell that was thrown into a truck full of 40 people and the resulting capture; "Several captives were kicked down from the truck and shot to death." In all the fighting that month, he said, over 500 people in his hometown were killed, and five of the leaders were illegally tried and executed. In the month of August, as well, the People's Liberation Army (PLA) intervened to help some intellectuals of the Dongfang Hong faction to escape to surrounding counties. Ultimately, through the years of 1968 and 1969, the two factions were forced to negotiate through the mediation of the army.

The tale of this grisly battle where people were beaten with steel bars, or captured, or shot had, of course, a tremendous impact on my class. However, they were most interested in finding out this student's role in the fighting. He maintained that he had simply been an observer, keeping post on a hill overlooking the battle scene, and that he had not taken part in it.

"But you were an active member of Dongfang Hong, weren't you?" insisted one student.

"Of course," he replied.

"Well, then, you must have taken part."

"No, I didn't," he insisted. "I was in the town, and one of my classmates came and told me that a battle was about to happen, and so I went to see, because I wanted to see how a real battle was."

"Come on — out with the truth," yelled one student. "How many people did you kill that day?"

I was shocked at this outburst, and yet no one else, including the student giving the report, was at all ruffled. The student simply maintained, again, that he had not participated in the fighting at all.

This is the sobering kind of report that impinges on the approval for the aims of the Cultural Revolution that I brought with me to China, and that I keep trying to bring up to my students. They often, but not always, agree with me that the aims were sound, but they always point out that things got "out of control." Today I got the feeling that I was being given a small lesson in what "out of control" meant.

DIARY ENTRY
Wednesday, August 20

On Saturday, one of the students in Ian's class who is leaving the course early to do an assignment in Beijing came to say goodbye to us. We began talking about the problem of classroom discipline in China, something that touched on a seminar Ian and I had given to the two classes on the methodology of speaking. Ian had delivered a sermon on the importance of teachers listening to other teachers, because he'd noticed a tendency on the part of the students to "turn off" when other students were speaking. One of the students responded with some force, "In 1965, Chairman Mao called on the students to doze in class, or to read something else if they found what the teacher was saying was boring. So now we teachers have no right to demand the students' attention." That, I thought, was that on the question of student inattention until I looked up Mao's conversation with his niece to remind myself of the context. And I smiled with pleasure at his inflammatory words, remembering their effect on me when I'd first read them as a student over ten years ago. The niece was complaining of a cadre's son who dozed and read fiction in class, and Mao responded by chiding her for being afraid of rebelling and upsetting the school system. Secretly, I approve of Mao's sentiments — it *is* right to rebel.

韓琳

DIARY ENTRY
Thursday, August 21

Today, Xiao Wang had the whole class in stitches throughout his oral report, which was on the topic of "Some Relations in a Chinese Family." He started out by saying that he was going to discuss a problem that is common in China's 300 million families — that of "soft-eared men." We would translate this as the "hen-pecked husband" phenomenon. Immediately my hackles were raised.

"Ninety-nine per cent of the men in my apartment building are afraid of their wives," he stated.

"Including you?" one student asked.

"No, *except* me," he answered. "When I got married, at first I was afraid of my wife, and she tried to tell me what to do. But I gave her a tit-for-tat struggle. So that's how I realized that women are paper tigers. Nothing to be afraid of."

I grimaced.

He went on to say that in most Chinese families, there is conflict between the husband's wife and his mother; but that most Chinese men are so afraid of their wives, that, given a choice, they would rather offend their mothers. The people in the class tried to discount his own claims of being free of "soft-eared-ness" by questioning his closely on how much housework he does at home. "I do *some* housework," he answered, keeping the amount a secret, and going on to say that the more housework a man did, the clearer the evidence that he was afraid of his wife. He was obviously doing his best to bait the women, and one of them fell right into the trap, by taking him seriously.

"How can you jump into such a conclusion?" she cried, exasperated. It reminded me of Miss Li's titters about Jiang being a "model husband"; there must be a standard joke about a husband who helps out above and beyond the call of duty, thereby calling his independence into question.

This evening, when two of the women in the class were here visiting, I asked them what they had thought of Wang's report, and told them that it was my impression that younger Chinese husbands did, generally, a lot more housework than husbands in North America. I told them I thought that was a good thing. They agreed, and said that on the whole the men did do their share, and this kind of joke didn't bother them.

However, one woman went on to point out that if both the husband and wife were professors, they had an equal amount of preparation and schoolwork to do. But, she said, the wife would tend to put her own work second to her husband's, and the result was that she wouldn't advance as rapidly. "It's a *very* serious problem in the

universities," she said grimly, and the other woman
agreed.

韓琳

Friday, August 22
Dear Peter and Cathy,

I wanted to wait until I had time to write a decent letter
to you two because we got to see the Qin Shih Huang
tombs, the 2200-year-old "spirit city" that you mentioned
to me, Peter, before I left. This was the site near Xian that
some peasants digging a well in 1972 accidentally discovered. It's estimated that it holds 6000 six-foot-tall terra
cotta warriors.

These life-size soldiers and the horses were spectacular,
although I was thoroughly distracted when I was looking
at them by a violent desire to take photographs, which
wasn't allowed. I kept seeing all these wonderful shots —
a single bare hand, unearthed and cleaned and sticking
out of one of the walls that keeps the rows of soldiers in
file. Or the people working down in the rows: they were
digging out more statues (there are enough figures of
horses and men there to keep them digging for 20 years)
and filling small baskets with earth and hoisting the
baskets out with a pulley, after carefully sifting away all
the red clay. If you've seen the TV program on it, you
know the site is now housed in a huge hangar-like
building — though, Chinese-style, you can never really
keep the elements out of the indoors, and I saw birds in
the rafters!

What amazed me about all this was the fact that the
technology existed 22 centuries ago to allow such
marvellous pieces of art to be produced — all the artisans
and kilns and metallurgy for the weapons and the enamel
paint (though that's worn away by now). This emperor,
Qin Shih Huang, is significant in Chinese history, though
his role has recently undergone a re-evaluation. He

essentially unified China, and is the emperor responsible for joining together all the sections of the Great Wall. You probably remember from your childhood the stories of how many people died building that, and how their bones were built into the wall. But the Chinese now call him "progressive" because, in consolidating the empire, he's credited with doing away with a stage of feudalism. He was not actually the one to do away with the inhumane practice of burying soldiers alive with an emperor to guard him in the after-life, but he chose to symbolize the practice by burying clay soldiers instead. He conscripted an army of 700,000 artisans, potters, painters and labourers, who worked 36 years to produce this "spirit city."

After his death, some group or individual or bandits set fire to the wooden structure that these soldiers were "housed" in; so that it, and the 15 or 20 feet of earth piled on top of it collapsed, and this ultimately preserved the whole thing. His tomb, however, is in another site, which has been known about and visited for a long time.

Cathy, you asked about the role of kids in this society. An enormous question. But, a brief attempt. Children here are called "the flowers of China," and they're cherished and loved by everyone. In this respect, China reminds me of Ireland, where everyone seems to know how to take care of kids, instead of having some weird ideas that they're hard to relate to, like lots of people in North America feel. But now the One Birth Movement has taken place, and in the cities, well over 90% of the women of childbearing age have taken a pledge to have only one child. In the countryside, the peasants are swinging into this a little more slowly. It's the typical rural Third World outlook: a male child is valued more than a female, for feudal-sexist reasons but also because of cold hard economics. A male child, when he grows up, can take care of elderly parents, unlike a female, who marries into another family. So many peasants want to retain the right to try and try and try until a baby boy comes along. Of course the solution is some kind of pension or guaranteed income for the retired (people basically don't retire until they're no longer able to work; there are 80-year-old professors in our department) and some of the wealthier, high-productivity communes (like the model brigade we were taken to visit) can afford to offer people this kind of insurance. So in these wealthier places, the number of women taking the pledge to have only one child is higher. But it's hard on the Chinese. *Everyone* gets married, usually by 28 and everyone wants a child. It's a source of great grief if a couple can't have one. The uniformity of the marriage-child process amazes me, and of course this means that no one can figure out why we aren't married. At our ages. And we can't give satisfactory answers...

DIARY ENTRY
Friday, August 22

I can't remember how my student and I got onto the topic again, but when he was visiting last night, things inched around to the Cultural Revolution; this student is the one who allows himself to say the bitterest things about Chairman Mao, and he doesn't even agree with me that the aims of the Cultural Revolution were worthy.

"For example," he said, "the Chinese people have always been very, very loyal, and it was always the custom for the people to wish the Emperor a very long life, a hundred thousand years. And Mao had the people doing exactly the same kind of thing — saying "Long live Chairman Mao," and things like that. That's not a revolutionary practice, that's feudal. Do you know what we had to do every day during the Cultural Revolution? This was ridiculous — we had to stand in front of a picture of Mao and speak to the picture, criticizing ourselves. Whole families had to do it every day, even little children, stand in front of the picture and confess bad thoughts. That was foolishness."

"But don't you think people like you — intellectuals — are much more critical of the Cultural Revolution, and of Chairman Mao, than, say, the peasants are, because your experiences were so bitter? I mean, you were forced to leave your homes and your schooling, and go to the countryside, and you weren't always welcome among the peasants, and it was difficult to arrange returning to your home units. Don't you think that you are more sensitive and critical now because of those kinds of experiences?"

"No, not at all," he said, and then he asked me, "Do you mean that the peasants are less critical of Mao than we intellectuals?"

"Yes," I said, "that's what I would have thought."

"No!" he said, "they are *more* critical!"

"More critical!" I laughed, "I can't believe it!"

"Yes, it's true. Do you know what happened one time when I was in the countryside working with the peasants, when I was assigned to a commune?"

"No, what?" I prodded.

"We had been working hard all morning, and it was very, very hot, and were taking a break inside a small hut. I was the only 'educated youth' there; the rest of the men were the peasants of the commune. We were exhausted, and we still had lots more work to do. One of the old men looked at the picture of Mao on the wall, and got very angry. He said to the picture, 'Look at you! With a nice suit, well-fed, sitting in a nice chair! And look at me — dirty, with these old clothes all worn out and ripped, and tired, and working hard all day, all my life!' And then he spit at the picture."

"Oh my God!" I exclaimed. "Did anything happen to him for doing that?"

"No," replied the student. "There were no leaders there, and no one told anyone what he'd said."

Saturday, August 23
Dear Penny,

Well, Saturday night, had a hot bath a minute before the water went off, changed the sheet (yes, I have only one), trimmed my toenails, and the mosquitoes are biting my freshly-bathed and scented ankles.

If nothing else, I have learned on this trip the relation between being tired all the time, getting sick and being forced to sleep. In order to get everything done I want to get done, or enjoy doing, like writing letters, I always stay up late and usually miss the noontime nap. Then I get a cold. Now I have my fifth cold since I arrived. Gripe, moan, sniffle.

You've quit smoking! Bravo! There's a lot of anti-smoking propaganda and only two or three of our students smoke (no women; only old ladies smoke among the female sex). Even the smokers think that we're heavy smokers. Cigarettes are expensive in relation to the salaries here; and the men get lots of flack from their wives over this costly and filthy habit. The anti-smoking campaign is apparently much less effective among the peasants.

We are mulling over a moral crisis. We have to write final reports on all our students, and in the main, this is just a chore. But for one or two of our students who haven't done a stroke of work — most are strikingly conscientious — we have to choose our words carefully. Salaries and eventual promotions depend on things like our reports, and the students are therefore quite anxious about them. Today in class, one student asked me *not* to type his. He explained that if I typed it, some unfavourable things could be typed in at the end by some ill-wishing leader. Even the other students thought this request was a bit paranoid, but this student stuck to his guns, so I promised to hand-write them all. This is, in a way, another legacy of the Cultural Revolution, when teachers' careers stood or fell on the basis of a criticism by someone in authority over them. The thing that bothers me about the few who have done so little work is that they feel because they have always been considered "bright," they don't merit any criticism. We are just keeping the two or so who are petrified of a poor report dangling — no reassurances — which is, I think, punishment enough, given their level of anxiety.

I think I mentioned to you in one of my first letters that the campus appeared to have been destroyed, and that I was told that a lot of damage was done to the buildings during the Cultural Revolution. It's funny, the changes that take place in one's perceptions when one gets accustomed to a place. Now that I'm used to it, Sichuan University doesn't at all seem to carry signs of damage. There is a lot of construction going on, but that's quite a different thing. And I have found out that there wasn't, in fact, any damage done to the buildings during the Cultural Revolution. But, to account for the fact that I was told there was damage: I guess people were sort of embarrassed that I perceived the campus as run-down and simply hastened to murmur assent when I asked if there had been a lot of destruction in those years. Interesting. Another example, too, of the tendency to blame the Cultural Revolution for problems that would exist in any case. It's hard to maintain the buildings in tip-top condition when there is a national shortage of things like paint, nails and concrete. Finding a nail is like finding a gold coin: I have a little supply of five or six, all different sizes, none of them new, that I have scrounged. Habits change, perceptions change (and so does information).

You asked if we knew what the Chinese people did when they went home at night. Well, here you can actually *see* what Chinese people do at night, at least in the summer, because it's so hot that much of evening family life takes place outside. Everybody takes chairs and sits around in little circles in the courtyard and chats with neighbours, plays cards (boys, men, old ladies only). Women do their knitting walking around, which I find remarkable. The little boys play a game which is sort of like "gambling" with old cigarette packages. Everyone supervises the kids, whose games divide along sex lines, just like ours did when we were small. . .

DIARY ENTRY
August 23

Ran across a Chinese proverb translated in a student's diary: "The grass can't be burned out by a prairie fire but grows again with the spring breeze." I was struck by how much it seemed like a response to Mao's famous old saying, "A single spark can start a prairie fire."

DIARY ENTRY
August 24

I am very proud of my new acquisition, which is a recipe for a dish that I love: *Mapo Doufu*. Last night, a teacher in the department invited us over to his house with the express purpose of teaching me how to make it. The full name means "Pock-marked Granny Chen's Beancurd," and the dish dates back to the 1860s. A certain Ms. Chen managed to marry a man who ran a restaurant in Chengdu, despite her pock-marked face. They were very happy for a brief year only, and then, tragically, he died. She continued to run the restaurant for many years. One day, she found the restaurant full of hungry soldiers — and she, with only *doufu* on hand! The dish she put together in this emergency became an instant hit, and the restaurant still thrives in Chengdu.

Here's the recipe that Li Guolin and his wife, Wu Yisha, use; I jotted it down as we cooked it:

- Soak *doufu* (beancurd) that has been chopped up in ¼-inch cubes in boiling water (this only heats it) and drain. Do this a couple of times as you attend to the rest of the cooking.
- Add ⅓ cup of oil to the wok; when it's hot, throw in 1 tsp. of salt.
- Dump in ⅓ pound of ground pork, and let cook in the oil.
- As the pork is cooking, add (in this order):

1. chopped garlic
2. ground *huajiao* (Sichuan peppercorns)
3. chopped ginger
4. oiled *lajiao* (these are dried red pepper flakes over which hot oil has been poured — a familiar condiment on Sichuan tables).

- Stir a fair bit after each addition, letting the spices cook through individually.
- Put in the chopped *doufu*, and add a little more salt, and about ¼ to ⅓ cup soy sauce and a tablespoon or two of malt vinegar. Again cook and stir gently after the addition of each spice. (After trying this recipe several times at home in Canada, I have found that 2 to 3 tablespoons of cornstarch mixed with 4 to 5 tablespoons of water and added at this point helps the dish reach its slightly thick, soupy consistency.)
- Cook for about 15 minutes over a good high heat.
- Sprinkle ground *huajiao* (Sichuan peppercorns) and chopped green onions on top of the dish (another refinement: a teaspoon or two of sesame oil at this point makes the dish aromatic) and serve over rice.

There are seven traditional flavours of Sichuan food: sour (vinegar), hot (peppers), "numbing" (the effect of Sichuan peppercorns), bitter (onions), sweet (honey or sugar), fragrant (garlic and ginger) and salty (soy sauce or salt). This dish is essentially a hot and "numbing" one, but most of the other flavours are present as well.

· FULL MOON ·

The poet Su Shi writes:

> At the Mid-Autumn festival in the year *ping-ch'en* (1076), I enjoyed myself by drinking until dawn and became drunk. I wrote this poem, thinking of Tzu-yu.

> To "Water Song"

> 'Bright moon, when was thou made?'
> Holding my cup, I ask of the blue sky.
> . . .
> Around the vermilion chamber,
> Down in the silken windows,
> She shines on the sleepless,
> Surely with no ill-will.
> Why then is the time of parting always at full moon?
> . . .
> All I can wish is that we may have long life,
> That a thousand miles apart we may share her beauty.*

The day of our departure from China was the first day of Mid-Autumn Moon Festival. In all the cities we had been visiting at the end of our stay in China, we had been reaping the benefits of the preparation for this festival by developing an addiction to *yue bing*, mooncakes. I had read of mooncakes long ago in Han Suyin's autobiographies, but had no idea of

---

* A.R. Davis, ed., *The Penguin Book of Chinese Verse*, trans. Robert Kotewall and Norman Smith (Harmondsworth: Penquin Books Ltd., 1968), p. 41.

how beautiful these intricately-stamped pastries were, or how delicious their savoury or sweet fillings could be. There is a very wistful note to the celebration of this festival, when, it was explained to us, "families sit out under the round moon, admiring it and eating mooncakes." This wistfulness corresponded with many of the feelings Ian and I were experiencing as we thought of leaving China.

At the end of the course at Sichuan University, our students were weary after a long summer of plugging at English while their own students and their colleagues were enjoying vacations. This weariness was something that Ian and I shared, for there had been only a couple of brief breaks from our intensive teaching duties. Many of the students, as well, were looking forward to returning to their families, and consequently the regret they felt at leaving Chengdu was balanced by that anticipation.

Several small ironies cropped up in our final weeks at the university. The most obvious one was that, just as we were leaving Chengdu, we felt closer than ever to our students. We were also beginning to manage our lives more and more capably, though hardly autonomously. For instance, for one of my last bike rides around the city, I had to borrow a bike since the student to whom I had sold mine had already shipped it back to his hometown; and, on this ride, I discovered a small bicycle rental shop. And of course we continued to find interesting new shops and pleasant teahouses on the final trips we took into town to do our last-minute shopping.

It seemed, also, that I was just starting to learn what, and how, the Chinese were debating politically. At the end of that summer, everyone was talking about the national plan to "retire" some of the old cadres with very generous pensions and new homes in their original villages. This was an unprecedented move in China, where one is supported until death by the unit, and where, consequently, few people fully retire. Many welcomed this plan, for it was seen as an attempt to ease out of power the older cadres blocking change; some, on the other hand, expressed concern at the extremely comfortable arrangements being offered these older cadres to entice them out of the units they had been in for thirty years or more. There was also the point of view that the target of this retirement plan might not simply be the ineffective, elitist cadres, but rather the original core of worker-, peasant- and soldier-based Party leadership who might be in opposition to modernization policies. For the first time, I got the sense of a concrete political debate in which people were taking different sides. It was gratifying to experience the discussion around this issue as a complexity of positions, rather than a unanimous "line," yet it was also frustrating to discover this complexity so late in my stay.

Another irony was the fact that we were leaving just as the rest of the campus came back to life. With the return of the students came the arrival of several new foreign experts, and one of the final duties we took on with pleasure was acquainting them as much as we could with the city and the unit. We were sorry to be missing the chance to spend a year working with them. So while the rest of the campus was plunging into the new school year, Ian and I were frantically busy with our final reports and interviews, our closing ceremonies and farewell banquets. We had a sense of not exactly doing things right, of being out of rhythm, of leaving just as everyone else was arriving.

Throughout our last days in Chengdu, the astonishing kindness and generosity of our colleagues and students gave us a curious mixture of regret and anticipation. Our excitement was not so much due to our thoughts of home, although they were certainly part of it, as to our hopes for our upcoming trip through China.

The expectations I had of the trip were that the rest of China would come into focus, and I would finally understand the regional differences that the people around us so frequently spoke of: "Guilin is the most beautiful part of China," "People in Shanghai are friendlier and more sophisticated," "The weather in Yunnan is much nicer than in Sichuan," "The provinces in the interior of China are poorer and more backward than the coastal ones." I had an intense curiosity about whether or not what we had seen and experienced in

Chengdu could be generalized to the rest of China. I was particularly anxious to broaden our contacts and to talk to people who were not intellectuals, who worked outside the context of a city.

Of course, some of these hopes proved to be unrealistic. I realized that a tourist in China often travels in an isolation that is imposed not in order to prevent contact, but to afford more comfort, as a privilege. Tourists may wander as freely as they wish through the cities of China, yet requests to do things like eat in a "mass restaurant" are viewed not so much with alarm, as with puzzlement. The sense of isolation from the ordinary life of the Chinese was, to a certain extent, lessened for us by meeting up with former students in three of the four cities we visited. There we spent time with people who understood perfectly our desires to travel in public buses rather than private cars, to linger over meals rather than rush off to the next tourist sight, to shop in the ordinary Chinese stores as well as in the special ones set up for foreigners. As we encountered the new bureaucratic entanglements of arranging our trip, we laughed and reminisced about the old ones at Sichuan University.

One surprising feature of our final month in China was the function it served in reintegrating us into Western culture. Leading the lives of tourists and viewing closely the lives of the journalists and diplomats in the cities gave us small but successive doses of culture shock. Each encounter with a formerly familiar comfort, like a hot shower or a telephone conversation with a friend, gave us the sense that we were truly "going out." In each city that we visited, it seemed, more Western amenities were available than in the previous one; and with each step that we took away from Chengdu, the increasing availability of Western comforts was something we had to get accustomed to.

Although our tour through China was the most fascinating and illuminating trip in my life, I returned to Canada with many questions still unanswered, and of course, so much of the country still unknown.

I think there are very few people who return from China who do not want to go back for an even longer time, and I am no exception. As my stay drew to a close, I became more and more certain that I would return to China, and I began to contemplate how I would do things differently "the next time." I was painfully aware of my naiveté and my unpreparedness: it seemed shocking to have been sent to China with only a month's conscious, explicit preparation. Of course, the first and most important task would be to arrive knowing much more of the language, because without being able to speak and listen and read, one is not only reduced to child-like dependence, but one is simply not able to take advantage of opportunities for contact and assimilation. In the area of political preparation, a good deal of in-depth reading of recent reports and histories of China is a sufficient base on which to begin building that most important of skills — knowing which questions to ask. It had taken me more than a month to realize that the Chinese could no more answer my questions about what things were like during the Cultural Revolution than I could answer bald questions about what the Sixties were like in North America; developing an ability to ask specific and intelligent questions took time. In many ways, I feel that the best preparation I have for my "next time" is the time I have already spent in China, when I learned how important it is to be open and accessible and inquiring.

Now there are letters coming to me from China, from former students and the experts we made friends with in Chengdu. Some of my ongoing questions are answered in these letters, so that my curiosity about new developments and concerns is sometimes satsified. I was pleased, for example, to read of the outcome of an event which is recorded here and which took place in Chengdu during our last week at Sichuan University. In one of the first letters I received after I got home, Sharon Hare wrote about the scaffolding that had been put up around the Mao statue in Chengdu (China's largest statue of Mao): mysteriously, she reported, when the scaffolding was removed, there were "no discernible changes — Mao's features haven't been changed to Deng's." As with many outcomes in China, this turn of events raised as many questions as it answered. Was there originally an intention to destroy the statue? Did the leadership pull back on this decision at the last moment? Or was it a routine clean-up job? The letters from our students inform us of familiar concerns: getting a chance to study abroad, teaching under heavy schedules, missing access to foreign experts, using the techniques we taught them; there is almost always a teasing reference to our habits or the attack on clichés we surprised our students with, and each letter expresses the hope that we'll someday return. One student has even promised to meet us at the airport with *jaozi* and *doufu*!

Here, then are the experiences of our final month in China; most of the observations are made in the form of diary entries, because, in the last two weeks of our stay, any letter I wrote would have arrived in Canada after I did. And, I suppose, along with my hard-earned holiday from teaching, I needed to take a holiday from letter-writing, too.

韓琳

Monday, August 25
Dear Pat,

Right now I've woken up groggy from a rare noontime nap, have put on some coffee to boil (that's how I make it here) and have settled into letter-writing till we have to go to the department to have our class pictures taken. The final little ceremonies are being arranged and taking place — this is the last week of teaching and everything's all in a commotion. I have packed half a suitcase in an attempt to see if everything I want to take home will fit. We're giving away some of our books and the students are overjoyed at getting some new materials.

Han Suyin keeps re-entering my life. A woman on Mount E Mei told our wonderful Shanghai student, who was our interpreter for the trip, that I looked like Han Suyin (of course, all Westerners or half-Westerners look alike). And then last Sunday we were taken to a 2000-year-old irrigation system, just a little bit boring, and we passed through Han Suyin's hometown/birthplace...

DIARY ENTRY
Tuesday, August 26, 7:10 a.m.

So, so tired, bleary-eyed and sick, mucousy — but woke up at 6:20, amazingly, and so I thought I'd have a few minutes for myself till breakfast. Picking out clothes for the day, I discovered a rat under my dresser, this one's head smooshed in by the trap and blood spurted out of its eyes. An involuntary scream and then I went and whined to Ian, waking him up.

DIARY ENTRY
Tuesday, August 26

One of Ian's students was talking to me on Friday about buying one of our bicycles when we leave. She'd like to buy one of ours because, she explained, she is far down on the Foreign Language Department's list of people waiting for bicycle tickets. Without one of these tickets, you can't go to the store and buy a bike.

"How many names are there on this list?" I asked.

"About eighty," she answered. "And do you know how many tickets are sent to the Foreign Language Department?"

"No," I said, "how many?"

"Two every two years."

"My God! Some people might have to wait twenty years!" I said. "Why doesn't the government allow more bicycle production? It'd certainly be profitable."

"I don't know exactly, but I think it's because we need the steel for heavy industry."

I finally understood that the concern over bikes being stolen is more complex than just their expense, which is also considerable (about three months' salary for the average worker). The limited availability of bikes — which we hadn't experienced because bikes aren't rationed for foreigners — makes them all the more precious.

DIARY ENTRY
Wednesday, August 27

A windfall today: one of those spectacular kindnesses that people here show us after they find out a peculiar eccentric taste of ours. A few weeks ago, on an outing with some of our students, I expressed an interest in buying and taking home a Mao button, which was something missing from my collection of political buttons. The problem was, I said, they were nowhere to be found — wasn't there anywhere I could buy a Mao button?

The students laughed and some commented ruefully, "Oh, I wish you had told me earlier — I have *dozens* at home!" Today, at lunch, a student rushed into our dining hall with a package for me that he said arrived ten minutes earlier from his wife. When I opened it, my eyes popped: there were 40 Mao buttons of various sizes pinned onto an old handerchief.

"You can't give us all these!" I protested. "I just wanted *one*! This is far too much to give me!"

And the student protested in turn, "No, no, no, you must have them — I really have no more use for them, and besides, this isn't all I have; I have even more at home. When I heard you wanted them, I wrote my wife and got her to send just a few. I'm so glad they've arrived in time, before you left."

The exchange of protests finally ended, of course, in my accepting them with astonishment and delight. And then, later that afternoon, Ian told his class how pleased I was. Some of the students shook their heads grimly and expressed surprise that I would even be interested in them.

"It's crazy," one student said. "We all have collections that big of Mao buttons. And we used to wear them, too. Sometimes we'd wear ones as big as a soupbowl. It was just crazy, all those buttons."

Amidst the general dismay at remembering this custom, one student spoke up.

"You know," he said, "Chairman Mao never liked the custom either."

"Oh, that's not true," the others scoffed. "He *said* he didn't like it, but why did he permit it? He could have stopped it if he'd wanted to."

"It *is* true," the lone student insisted. "He used to say that many airplanes could have been made from all the Mao buttons that people were wearing. And one day, when he was greeted by a lot of people wearing the buttons, he got very angry and said, 'Give me back my airplanes!'"

I got the impression that the story fell into the open air, convincing no one but chiding everyone with the facts.

韓珠

DIARY ENTRY
Thursday, August 28

In my life, I have never had such a day. Things happened at a fuse-blowing pace, not necessarily in this order:

1. Jiang's wife had a baby at 7:30 this morning — a boy, seven jin point two in weight, whatever that is.
2. I interviewed 13 students in a row for half an hour each, gruelling farewells, with chaotic interruptions having to do with —

3. Ian's getting *very* sick, a mysterious ailment much more serious than a cold. So sick that he agreed to see a doctor, and I communicated that to Miss Li, and she arranged for a car to take him to the Sichuan Medical College. Then, when the driver arrived, he perversely refused to go, claiming he was much better. So then she told me she was going to bring two doctors from the clinic on campus (whispering from 50 feet away to to me on Ian's balcony, "Don't tell him!" and me saying, "I won't!"). And then the two doctors arrived and left a myriad of pills that I administered at regular intervals throughout the day because Ian was too sick to figure out what to take and when to take it.

4. Comrade Li in the kitchen arranged a *jiaozi* (dumpling) lesson for me, and I asked the Endicotts, and we all had a wonderful time, making them and eating them. Poor Ian, couldn't even appreciate *jiaozi*.

5. Some big fight occurred over our final return banquet, the one Ian and I are giving the leaders and workers of the university. One leader refused to arrange something, and Miss Li blew up.

6. The students held their farewell party for us tonight, and Ian couldn't attend; it was a beautiful affair, very warm, with lots of fun and laughter, and a shower of gifts that astounded me. I suppose I was most touched by the Four Precious Things, the ink and slab and brush and stand that are used for Chinese calligraphy.

7. A separate accomplishment: I sang a song, solo, at the party (something that I, with my wretched voice, have never done before). It was "The Frozen Logger," which everybody thought was pretty weird; it is, but at least it's Canadian.

8. I wrote 11 reports on my students for them to take back to their colleges.

9. I had a heart-to-heart with the dean of the FL Department at the party.

10. I gave away about 30 of my books to my students.

11. I nursed Ian as best I could through all of this.
12. And I sold my bicycle.

韓琳

DIARY ENTRY
Friday, August 29

This is the date that has been etched in all our minds — the last day of classes. Of course, it was anti-climactic, and strangely unlike our usual routine. Since Ian was sick, I had to take both our classes, and that meant I had to keep zipping back and forth between the two. We were assigning a final composition, to be done in class, which the students persisted in seeing as an examination, although we had told them time and again that we were only doing it for form's sake, because of the leaders' requests. Their "final marks" were to be their reports, which they knew I had already written. They could not be calmed down on this score. They were also taken a bit aback by the topic for the composition: "What do you think is the greatest problem facing China?"

韓琳

Saturday, August 30
Dear Mary Ellen, Neil and Joanne,

I have the same ambivalence you did, Mary Ellen, about leaving. Now that the Endicotts are here, and we've got Sharon at the next university, I keep thinking how good it would be to be working here through the winter. And this Stephen Endicott has such a lot of information, stuff I'd never in 20 light years hear from the Chinese. As a kid, he lived in Leshan (remember the big Buddha) and he always spent his summers climbing E Mei.

Ian got very sick last week (he's now recovered) — a flu thing with — fever-chills-sweat. So sick he couldn't attend the farewell party the students held for us. Nor could he attend the "return banquet" we gave the honchos. Both were sort of distressing to experience, especially alone; the first because we were showered with extravagant presents and very, very touching farewells that got me all choked up. The second because we were forking out over 100 yuan and the "guests" sat around talking in Chinese the whole night without paying a shred of attention to me. The killer was the heated discussion they had about how expensive foreign experts were and how they couldn't get any subsidy from the ministry for things the interpreters spend on us. (Like what?) Well, I suppose this is the stuff of which culture shock is made: things that we think are rude, unbearably so, are not rude here. Yes?

Ian really was in bad shape: he couldn't even count out the pills he was supposed to take. Of course, Mary Ellen will remember this is no mean feat — three of these at one time, one of these, four of those. He refused to have any injections or even to go to the doctor's, so everybody, including the president at the banquet, got their shirts in a knot over how "childish" (not an insult in Chinese) he was. At one point he made me promise that if he died I wouldn't bury him in China, like Norman Bethune, but in front of Mars [a Toronto greasy spoon, famous for its breakfasts]. I agreed and said I would daily place a buttered bran muffin and two styrofoam cups of coffee, double cream, on his grave. At the mention of double cream, he fell into a swoon.

Steve Endicott says the definition of an expert here is "someone who's far away from home." And now Sichuan University is rolling in new experts: besides the Canadian Endicotts, there are two 22-year-old women from the University of Virginia, who have no teaching experience. Hmm. Then there's another American, a guy, a mountain climber whom I haven't met yet. He of course will make it to the top of E Mei in a minute flat.

Well, comrades, this is one wiped out *waibin* about to sign off.

DIARY ENTRY
August 30

I realized with amazement today that I haven't
mentioned in any of my letters home or even here in my
diary one notable response my body has made to this
whole experience: I haven't had a period since I came to
China. I am taking this as evidence that I have not yet
recovered from my culture shock. I have talked to Sharon
about it, and she says she didn't get a period for her first
three months here.

Sunday, August 31
Dear Aline and George,

Ahhhhh. Classes are finished, and this past week was,
if you can imagine it, even more hectic than my week
prior to departure in Canada (and you remember how
calm I was then!).

I have been given a huge mounted painting (and so has
Ian) — about eight feet long and three feet wide — mine
is of an ancient couple dancing. The student got the artist
to do this for us, so our Chinese names are written on
them. I met the artist; he is an amazing person. He works
in a hydroelectric factory, and has been asked to teach in
the Beijing Fine Art Institute, but refused because he
wanted to work "among the people." However, he has
recently agreed to a transfer to the Sichuan Print Shop,
here in Chengdu. I think that this kind of attitude is rare,
especially among younger people; he's quite young and
apparently famous. Our student got in touch with him
simply by writing him a letter. In return, I gave him two
art books (*Late Modern Art* and *Impressionist Paintings
in the Louvre*, which I bought in Paris in '68). I was quite
fond of these books, but he was stunned with pleasure
and gratitude when I gave them to him. The only

problem is that in order to have a proper place to hang this lovely painting, I will have to buy a house.

It cost me six yuan to have a sweater hand knit (less than $5); the wool cost about $18. And then I horrified Miss Li by having a *qipa*, one of those old lady blouses (frogs at the side, high neckline) made in plain blue cotton. She informed me in her primmest manner that her grandmother used to wear that kind of blouse, but the family "persuaded her to modernize." Then, in a last-ditch attempt, she brought the matter up again, saying the second time that they had *forced* her grandmother to discard these clothes and wear "modern" clothes. It was quite reckless of me to have something with a mandarin collar made, a sign of a feudal mentality on my part...

DIARY ENTRY
August 31

Got up at 7:21 despite my determination to sleep in. The cock crowed 99 times. I've been looking over our students' final compositions, and here's an informal survey of what they think is the greatest problem facing China:

- 11 out of 33 think it's overpopulation;
- ten out of 33 think it's "bureaucracy politics," "democratization" and the cadre system, typified by these kinds of remarks: "how to do away with the present cadre system," "cadres keep their posts all their lives, and one or two of them decide for the majority, with no full democracy," "because the cadres are mainly appointed by cadres of higher position, not elected, there is not full democracy among the people and exists a lot of red tape";
- four people think it's the speed and efficiency of production;

- three think it's education; there is some concern for "teachers' salaries and status" but mostly for modernizing the educational system.

  These problems got one vote each:
- science and technology;
- "how to raise people's enthusiasm";
- "raising the cultural level";
- poverty;
- youth "seeking everything foreign and poisoned by unhealthy popular songs."

One sentence caught my eye: "A well-organized government will bring all the Chinese people the greatest happiness."

Monday, September 1
Dear Carole,

You, my dear, are the first in the outside world to know that our request to go to Lhasa has finally been approved! Today's Monday and I think we should be going on Saturday for three days. It will cost a bundle, about $700. All I hope is that I don't get sick — we've been constantly warned about how "thin" the air is. "Roof of the world," here we come!!

Life is all hectic and jam-packed with big events lately. *Five* new English experts have arrived at Sichuan University and we feel like old hands, showing them the ropes the way Michael did for us. One couple, the Endicotts, are very interesting — his grandfather and father were both missionaries to China, he himself was born here, so he is steeped in China information that we're getting bits of. His father is famous in China, and his wife is an artist...

DIARY ENTRY
Tuesday, September 2

Today I gave my lecture on women to the whole university community. I suggested the idea of a final lecture as a ceremony to mark our departure. The leaders, to my surprise, were not thrilled, but a little stumped about how to set it up. That made me slightly impatient, because they had certainly known how to organize one for Michael Gasster when he was leaving. "You know how," I persisted, "just arrange for a big hall so that lots of students can come, and put up a few signs in English and Chinese, inviting everyone to attend, and telling them when and where it will be."

"But what will the title of your lecture be?" they asked, as if this was a major stumbling block.

"How about 'The Women's Movement in North America?' "

"Uh, well..." Their reluctance made me try another title.

"Well, how about just 'Women in North America?' "

"Oh, yes, that would be much better," they agreed. "We'll call it that."

So, a few days ago, signs went up all over the campus announcing this event — I didn't see them, and the Endicotts had to point them out to me. I started getting very nervous about what precisely I was going to say, and polled all our Chinese friends and students about what they'd want to hear in such a lecture.

Li Xingui was the most helpful. "We want to hear three things," he said. "We want to hear how women in North America work, how they live and how they love."

"Fine," I said, "That's great. That'll be my outline, and I'll mention that it was your suggestion."

The lecture went extremely smoothly. After pointing out some examples of sexism in the English language, I made a little introductory joke by changing the first point in my outline on the blackboard from "history" to "herstory." Everyone was delighted that they *got* the joke!

Under "herstory," I talked about some of the feminist causes I've helped take up. I went on to explain sexism by comparing it to racism, pointing out the systematization of privilege that maintains the exploitation of one group by another. Under "how women work," I explained how women and children were among the first factory workers in our society, and moved on to the present, noting that equal pay is still far from reality and that women are concentrated in non-unionized sectors. "How women live" led me into the double day and facilities like child care, and the problems of single mothers. I also talked about politics and the representation of women in Parliament; and I touched on other areas like sports, education and medicine. "How women love" was of course the most difficult because I found it impossible to generalize about North American women's attitude to love, except to state that almost all of us think it's very important. I talked about divorce in our society, something the Chinese have a lot of difficulty comprehending.

However, the best part of the lecture was the question period. I was pleased that I had made use of the technique suggested by Michael Gasster — giving out little slips of paper for questions — because it is much less intimidating than asking a question out loud in English. I got a flood of written questions and invited Sharon up on stage to help answer them. I think her participation was probably an unprecedented action, which startled the head of the department, because Sharon's university and ours are old rivals. There hasn't been much cooperation between them since the Cultural Revolution.

Here are some of the questions we were asked:
• Do the women who are engineers in North America have time to take care of their child and do their housework in their spare time? My wife is an engineer,

and she worries that she doesn't have time to do all this. (Note the assumption that a woman would have only one child.)

• Are there any women in the Mafia? If there are, what kind of jobs do they take charge of?

• What is the percentage of women who smoke in North America?

• What's the main reason that makes the family in North America split?

• Do you know how men react to the women's movement?

• What are the laws protecting a woman who is sexually attacked?

• Are there any married men and women who remain childless all their lives?

• The only "job" of a married woman is to satisfy her husband, isn't it?

• Compare the North American woman's attitude to love with that of the Chinese woman's, please.

• What are the standards that the North American women have in choosing husbands?

• If a wife has no work, how can she live on after being divorced by her husband?

• Do women have the same privileges of going to university or doing the same kind of work as men in North America?

• What part does the lesbian movement play in the North American women's movement?

Both Sharon and I were astonished by the question on lesbianism, because we were sure that very few people had even heard the term in English, and so we defined it. Sharon also gave a good explanation of the relationship between the women's movement and lesbianism.

At the end of the lecture, I gave out some women's buttons and feminist magazines to the women leaders of the university, and to some of the women students. Although they enjoyed the lecture and were delighted with the buttons and magazines, I ended up feeling somehow dismayed. It was as if I was caught in the wordless stretch between my own culture, which I can now see with Chinese eyes, and Chinese society. I was reminded of a quote in Sharon's book, *Quotes and Queries*: "To leap you have to be running" — I feel as if I'm still stumbling along, nowhere near running and very far from leaping into a real understanding of China.

Monday, September 8
Dear Betty and Colm,

We got very, very close to getting to Tibet — we even had tickets for a flight but our permission was revoked — and finally, we were not very surprised or disappointed. We were determined not to believe our good fortune till we got out of the car which takes you from the airport to Lhasa itself. Good thing we'd put ourselves in this frame of mind.

So this little break after teaching and doing final reports and all the packing we got done before going to Lhasa has given us time to (a) relax and (b) get to know the new experts at Sichuan University. On the one hand, I'd like to stay now that there is such a "huge" foreign ghetto, as we've begun to call ourselves. A lot of the pressure of extra work would be off us, and I'm sure we could get some excellent work done, pooling our resources. On the other hand, they've got a hard winter ahead of them — with the cold and damp and no central heating.

I forgot to tell you that Emer's presents for me were well used. You remember the "1th," "2th," "3th," "4th" and "5th" ribbon prizes she gave me for handing out to my students? And of course you remember the Mount E Mei trip? When we got back, I made up silly awards (Leader of the Shaky Legs Brigade Award, the Steady

Rock Award, the Merciful Monkey Award, etc.). I stuck Emer's prizes on the award papers and explained from whence they came. The students were charmed and thought they were wonderful!

We had a round of final banquets and farewell parties and were showered with presents, many extraordinary things, in particular, some exquisite paintings and calligraphies. Some were a little not-to-my-taste (in China, all that is bright and plastic and new is beautiful; all that is natural is old-fashioned and ugly).

Well, this is the last letter you'll be getting from this exotic city in the heart of southwest China.

韓琳

DIARY ENTRY
Tuesday, September 9
The wee hours

A touching moment in the dining hall: Comrade Li came up to our table at lunch and announced to Steve Endicott that we'd be having one of our favourites, *xiao baozi* (small steamed dumplings), for dinner tonight, as well as *duck*! This was the result of our saying how cheap chicken is in North America — it's a *very* expensive meat here — and how expensive, and therefore prized, duck is back home. And then she invited me to a *baozi*-making lesson in the kitchen before dinner. That was so nice; every few minutes, some comrade's arms were around me, correcting my dumpling-making technique, and Comrade Li kept looking at me, tracing tears on her cheeks and then laughing. She has been such a pleasure to know; I feel as if she's been a lifeline to the pleasant, dedicated workers I expected to encounter in China, and her wonderful manner really balanced the encounters with the wary, embittered and the uncaring.

韓琳

September 9
No change in place
Dear Janet,

Well, a sad and happy day — our last — I think, I hope, in Chengdu. I borrowed Ian's bike this afternoon while he took a nap — mine's long since gone to Kunming with the student I sold it to — and rode around, saying goodbye to the spots that have become familiar: the Worker Peasant Soldier Department Store, the Café Vienna, the Jin Jiang Hotel, Dung Feng Road and Shensi Road, the Children's Department Store, the poster store, the river park.

Tonight we dropped in on Comrade Jiang, one of our interpreters. This is something we've never done, but someone took us looking for the woman Ian's selling his bicycle to. She wasn't in but we discovered Jiang lived in the same building. We haven't seen hide nor hair of him, or any of our usual flock of friends for about two weeks (except at banquets) — but Jiang has a good reason. His wife just had a baby.

He was unprepared for us, of course, and all this took place in the middle of a power blackout. But we were ushered into his bedroom (they have *one* room for four of them — his wife, his mother, self and now baby) with one double bed and one single bed, two or three tables, a desk and a crammed bookcase. He apologized for "the poor conditions." They *are* poor. And the blackout made it all seem spookier and poorer. We sat down while his wife, a doctor, was breast-feeding, and Jiang and his mother rushed down the hall to the communal kitchen shared with two or three other families. They came back and gave us each a bowl of a traditional dish visitors get when they come to see a new baby: eggs poached in a startlingly sweet wine broth, with rice. It was a little hard to take, especially as we'd just eaten 500 dumplings each, a special favourite of ours that the kitchen people made for our Last Supper. Ian didn't touch it. But it's traditional to give a new mother eggs to eat — sometimes she'll get as many as 150 and she'll eat lots of them. But this must be the real way to get rid of all those eggs.

I held the baby, who was tiny and scrawny-necked. Jiang, stating the obvious as is the Chinese habit, but in his own peculiar English, said, "Sometimes it eats cow's milk, and sometimes it eats human milk." What I was thinking as I was holding this soaking wet baby wrapped very tightly in towels — they were *tied* on — was, "No brothers! no sisters!" because of the One Birth Movement.

We'll see Jiang and Miss Li and the leader who's made our lives a wreck and one who thwarted our trip to Lhasa tomorrow morning at 6 a.m. They'll see us off at the airport. That will be weird — remembering our arrival! Miss Li taught me my first Chinese word, *nihau* ("hello") then, and now I'm speaking in sentences. I have about nine verbs. I use them in all situations (sit, speak, go, give, eat, drink, like, want, be — that's it). Abominable progress. And me, a language teacher.

Right now I'm having a little shot of Chinese brandy which will undoubtedly make it even harder to get up in five hours. Ah, well.

So you've gotten my first letter from Chengdu and my last. It's been a hard summer, hard work, and I've had that grumpy feeling you get when you're working and everybody else is on vacation. I keep thinking that I've learned a lot less than I expected to, and that I haven't been able to absorb much from being here. But Sharon keeps assuring me that I'll be astounded when I get back at how intense the experience was and how much I took in unwittingly. Steve Endicott was here in 1975 when the country was fully enthusiastic about the Cultural Revolution; now of course there's only criticism of it, and the mood is much more negative. Sad. And something I joked about with Michael Gasster seems to have become a reality. "Just think," I said when I took a picture of him and his friend, Susan, in front of the enormous Mao statue downtown, "you'll be able to say you were in China when there were still Mao statues all over the place." Now, just last week, the Mao statue has had scaffolding erected around it and it'll be destroyed. China's changing — again. But you read about it in *Time* six weeks ago, right?

DIARY ENTRY
Wednesday, September 10
Kunming

Protested my way out of a Chengdu bed for the last time this morning — the approaching car, honking in the dark, woke Ian up at 5:55 and he woke me up. I raced around, throwing last-minute things into my bags; of course there was no water. I shook hands solemnly with the Dean of the FL Department, Lao Zhu, but Ian was much more awake and amiable, and then we sped away in the car with a retinue of people to see us off. We had a quick breakfast at the airport and sat around, making awkward small talk — thank God for Ian's sense of humour, which saves every difficult situation. Then it all happened very quickly — we were waved at, our hands shaken vigourously, I took some pictures and we were on the plane and it was lifting off.

And then Ian proposed taking the small flight gift — a fan with a picture of Mount E Mei on it — up to the cockpit and threatening the pilot that if he didn't take the plane to Lhasa, he'd be fanned to death.

So now the first "limb" of the homeward journey is accomplished, and we find ourselves holed up in an exquisite no-name hotel for cadres, not a *waibin* establishment, swanky in a Chinese way. It's in a quiet, walled area off a poor, narrow street (poorer, it seems, than Chengdu); but what makes Kunming so wonderful is the wide blue sky and blazing sun — it feels like early summer, not the cold and damp fall weather that was approaching in Chengdu.

It must be glorious to live in a city where the weather is always as lovely as this; Kunming is aptly called "The City of Eternal Spring."

DIARY ENTRY
Thursday, September 11
Kunming

It has been extremely pleasant to meet up with four of our students who are living and teaching here in Kunming. We gossiped late last night and tonight about bits and pieces of each other's lives, over mooncakes and coffee in the bar of the Kunming Hotel. We paid a price for keeping such late nights, though not as severe a one as did our students. They'd promised to get us back by ten o'clock, and we arrived back at eleven (it was, after all, the first night of our vacation!). We were greeted by the sight of Li Xingui (who's been sent with us by Sichuan University) fretting on the front steps of the hotel, and by Lao Hong, the cadre assigned to us by the Foreign Affairs office in Kunming, who was fuming. Lao Hong launched into a vicious dressing-down of the four students, and dismissed anything we had to say.

This cadre has earned everyone's intense dislike. When he asked us what visits we would like arranged, we said a factory, a hospital, a commune and especially some schools, including a Minority Nationality Institute. "No temples," I said, "we saw a lot of them in Sichuan." Well, he has refused to arrange most of these, but he might arrange the Minorities Institute. We have of course started calling the four students The Gang of Four because they have been blamed for all the problems by Lao Hong.

Lao Hong did arrange a trip to the Stone Forest, because he agreed this was essential. The Stone Forest is spectacular. It's one of those natural formations, like the Giant's Causeway in Ireland, that is seemingly inexplicable: a forest, yes, of very high jagged rocks jutting out of the ground. How did this come to be?

And everywhere we go in Yunnan, we see what is always noted about this section of China: the presence of 23 different national minorities. In the city, in the countryside, we often catch glimpses of colourfully dressed women with elaborate jewellery, walking along, or working, or selling.

Another difference we have spotted in the countryside is that you can occasionally see a small uncultivated patch of land, just a few bare yards by the side of the road. This is something you would never see in Sichuan — I suppose the needs of a hundred million in that one province mean that every square inch is used.

We're getting closer and closer to Western living. Today for lunch in our little hotel, we were served sliced tomatoes, which I just could not resist putting into my *mantou* with the fabulous Yunnan ham (it tastes like prosciutto) and making — heaven — a sandwich! We were, as well, astonished to be served a *salad* of lettuce; but, oh dear, it had a crunchy layer of white sugar sprinkled all over the top.

DIARY ENTRY
Friday, September 12
Kŭnming

We were up early and over to Yunnan University by eight o'clock this morning — a strange time to visit people, but the Gang of Four had worked out this pre-class time with the foreign experts at Yunnan

University and the Kunming Teachers' College. We had been hearing about Elizabeth Booz and her son, Paddy, and Steve Thorpe for months. And they had been hearing about us. In Chengdu, one of Ian's Kunming students told him that someone had gotten a letter from one of these experts, inquiring, among other things, whether Ian had found a Chinese wife yet. We were shocked but amused to find that Ian's joke (which all the students had initially taken seriously) had travelled so far.

The Boozes were as charming and interesting and energetic as all reports had indicated. They served us coffee and more mooncakes in their little house, a small bungalow with a front garden in a row of houses. And then they took us on a tour of the Foreign Language Department, where we were invited to sit in on a French class and an English class. We saw the language lab, which, unlike Sichuan University's, is functioning, and, wonder of wonders! piled up in the hall were boxes of tape recorders and equipment, imported from Japan, and about to be installed. We were also shown the English library, which the Boozes had set up through ongoing pleas for donations from people at home and from tourists passing through Kunming. Everyone was just-ifiably proud of the department and of the efforts of the Boozes.

Lao Hong, however, stepped out of his aloofness to rush us away, though we would dearly have loved to stay and have the tour of the rest of the campus. We made arrangements with the Gang to meet them for lunch in a restaurant downtown, another rendezvous which Lao Hong had nearly refused; it took some pleading and cajoling on the part of our students to wheedle permission out of him. "I told him that Ian was boring with the meals in the hotel," said Burma Li.

Chagrin is hardly the word for what we felt when we arrived at the destination Lao Hong had arranged for us. It was supposed to be a jade workshop, but it turned out to be exactly the same artisans' workshop that he had taken us to the day before! However, we were taken to a tiny stone-grinding section at the back that we hadn't already seen. A very kind older artisan gave me two or three unpolished stones, semi-precious, for my father, and waved away any offers for payment.

We met the Gang at a restaurant that serves a typical Yunnan specialty: a bowl of extremely hot broth into which is put thin slices of raw pork, sliced vegetables, "doufu skin" and rice noodles; a layer of oil on top keeps the broth hot so that it cooks the pork. We toasted with bowls of beer to Kunming, to Toronto, to the Gang of Four (scandalously), and to "*pengyou*-ship," and we had such fun that we decided to press our luck with Lao Hong and all meet for dinner that day, too.

After lunch and being taken back to our hotel, Ian and I took a wonderful walk through the streets near our hotel and along a river — we felt slightly naughty as Lao Hong and Li Xingui thought we were in our rooms, having a "good rest." We were back in time, though, to meet the car and to be taken to the Minority Nationalities Institute for the afternoon.

Li Xingui had gotten sick, and wanted to spend the afternoon in bed, but Lao Hong insisted that he come to the Institute. This was despite our protests that it wasn't necessary, as our students would be there to translate. No dice, said Lao Hong, and everybody was feeling the edge of grumpiness coming over us again; this man had such power over us. As we pulled up to the front gate of the Minority Institute, the driver spotted our four students and slowed down to let us out so that we could all walk into the Institute grounds together. But Lao Hong said imperiously to the driver, "*Zoule, zoule!*" ("Go on, go on!"), snubbing the students. When the car stopped further up the road, Ian and I stormed out of the car, slammed the door, and headed away from him as fast as we could to join our students. They were as offended as we were. I spoke to Li Xingui about this incident later, and told him that, in my eyes, Lao Hong had been very rude;

but perhaps a Chinese person would not see it as an offence? "No," said Li Xingui, "It was terribly rude." then, greeting the president of the Minorities Institute, Lao Hong didn't introduce the students until, wearily, I asked him to.

The usual routine of a visit: ushered into a *waibin* waiting room, served tea and given a "brief introduction" before a tour. The facts on the Minorities Institute: it was begun in 1958, suspended during the Cultural Revolution (1968) and not started up again until 1972, when Premier Zhou visited Kunming and noted the absence of an institute for the minorities. The president twinkled his way through his speech, a charming man, but both Ian and I wondered how the five minority students dressed in their beautiful costumes felt as he described their cultures as "backward." He told us of conflicts between the nationalities that occurred in the early days of the Institute, but now, he said, "they even fall in love with each other." This led us into a discussion of inter-marriage, and of the differences between the nationalities and the Han, the Chinese majority population. The president told us of an old saying — "As a pillow cannot be made with a stone, so a friend cannot be made with a Han."

There are now 600 teachers and 1000 students, but the leaders would like, over the next three years, to increase the number of teachers to 1000 and the number of students to 3000. As we left one building, a small door in the side of a hill caught my eye. "What's that?" I inquired.

"Uh, that hasn't been used for a long time," one of my students said.

"But what is it? It looks like an entrance to a shelter, a bomb shelter, or something," I persisted.

"Yes, that's what it is. We built these all over the universities in China during the Cultural Revolution."

"During the Cultural Revolution, or before, too?"

"Uh yes, well, before too," this student answered.

"But we had these at Sichuan University; didn't you ever see them there?"

"No," I said.

"Well, probably there are more here."

And then I remembered the consciousness in China during the mid-and late Sixties of the possibility of American attack; it was not totally far-fetched then, especially for the people of this province, which dips into Vietnam. In 1967, the United States announced its "anti-China" anti-ballistic missile, and in 1968, Chinese ships in a North Vietnamese harbour were bombed by American planes.

Later, after another delightful dinner, we met up with our car and driver, and had to say our final goodbyes to the Gang of Four. There was, of course, a crowd looking on. "You told me people didn't stare in Kunming," I said slyly to one of the students.

"They've come to say goodbye," he said, smiling.

DIARY ENTRY
Saturday, September 13
Guilin

Well, as Ian put it, much to Li Xingui's amusement, "China was liberated in 1949; Maureen and Ian were liberated this morning" — from the clutches of Lao Hong, that is. We left the hotel at six, driving through the darkened streets of Kunming; people were out on the streets, doing their morning exercises, one of them being a sleepy game of badminton under a streetlight.

We got on the 22-seat airplane with a crowd of overseas Chinese, and were served tea, not the usual fare given on airplanes, ice cream. Our flight gift was another fan. We read up on Guilin and Shanghai as the plane flew over a very mountainous area which then flattened out to agricultural lands out of which jut the distinctively weird mountains of Guilin.

A wonderful relief was in store for us: instead of a new boss, Lao Hong style, we were met by a competent young woman who was from the China Travel Service and who spoke English. She was perfectly willing to try to arrange everything we were interested in seeing.

A relief and an astonishment, actually. The hotel we were taken to, the Jiashang, is Australian-built, and our rooms contain the following amenities which we have not seen since we left Hong Kong: a bank of closets and cupboards, curtain racks, wall-to-wall carpeting, a naugahyde couch, continental beds (no mosquito nets), dimmer switches, a little Philips fridge, a built-in digital alarm clock/radio module between the beds. And how could I forget the air conditioning? All this put us into "comfort shock," and transformed us — Ian more drastically: he put on his white *waibin* pants, something only a Westerner would wear in China. I merely added a bit of jewellery, taking this change slowly. The transformation made Li Xingui laugh a lot.

In the afternoon, we went to see the Seven-Star Cave, a huge cave of stalactites and stalagmites. We came back for dinner in the hotel — shock of shocks! We were served tiny deep-fried baby birds with their heads and feet still on. "So these are the 'games' Xiao Jiang was talking about when I asked her about typical Guilin food," Ian commented. They were too disconcerting for words. These "rice birds" are, I believe, the acid test of an expert in China; they are of course a delicacy, but also the first food I've been put off by (no, I tell a lie: I'm forgetting the eels). We hid them behind the teapot on our table, and thanked the patron saint of banquets for having sent us this test when we were alone.

And during the air-conditioned night, my digital alarm went off at four o'clock — a steady hooting noise that put me on the ceiling, almost, disoriented.

DIARY ENTRY
Sunday, September 14
Guilin

Another early rising — what a holiday, no sleep, groaning out of bed, always late and rushing down to breakfast. Which was coffee (hurrah!), *youtiao's* (deep-fried non-sweet long doughnutty things, which we asked for), bread (warmed), butter (rancid), jam (fine), and a plate of cold fried eggs and luncheon meat.

Sprang into the car after getting double messages from Xiao Jiang: "We have *one* minute before eight; take your time." Then the car tore along the road to the debarkation point for the "ship" that was to take us on what Xiao Jiang referred to as a "river cruise."

And then such a calm, peaceful, blazing hot day followed. All the teaching difficulties, the administrative hassles, the worries and problems slipped quietly into the river and were left behind us. It was the quietest day we've spent in China; our boat was pulled, so even the sound of the motor was distant. The river and the surrounding mountains made this the most beautiful part of the world I've ever been in.

And I'd better not forget the Four Ultimate Beauties, which I tested Ian on last night, after giving him the Chinese-prepared booklet on the Li river.

Q. The Four Ultimate Beauties are enchanting hills, limpid water, fantastic caverns and dangerous shoals. True or false?

A. False. Dangerous shoals are not one of the Four Ultimate Beauties, while "wonderful rocks" are.

There was lots of life on the river, too — kids swimming, pulling or poling rafts upstream, water buffalo bathing, people crossing the river on small boats or waiting to be picked up on the shore, what seemed like a whole town of people wading in an inlet, fishing, other riverboats carrying cargo or tourists. It is supposed to be an 83-km journey, but we cut out early in order to be back in Guilin by three o'clock. The ideal way to arrange this trip is to go the full way down to Yangshuo, stay the night in a hotel there, and return the next day. That would be an even more splendid trip, but we were satisfied with ours.

DIARY ENTRY
Tuesday, September 16
Guilin

Today we devoted ourselves to the Chinese educational system, and had our visits to a kindergarten and to a middle school, and we were shown, naturally, a model kindergarten and a key middle school.

Guilin Middle School's "key" status, however, was taken away during the Cultural Revolution and not restored until 1978, after the downfall of the Gang of Four. We asked about this key school status. It is granted if the school has a long history, if the buildings and equipment are in good condition, and if its teaching groups are of high quality. Then, key status means that the school is sent the best graduates of the teachers' colleges, and can accept students with the highest marks (students with lower marks go to "common schools"). And it also means that you can apply for Foreign Experts. This seems somewhat of a Catch-22 situation.

Middle school begins for a Chinese youth at about age 12. In this middle school, there is a student body of 1200, divided into 27 classes, and there are 78 teachers, of 150 staff. Half of the students live at the school, and half of the students are female. The students take politics, Chinese, mathematics, physics, chemistry, biology, history, geography, English, sports, music and art. There are two general aims: to "nourish" college students, and to teach the students to make a contribution to socialism.

And, in fact, 51 per cent of the graduating class were sent on to university last year.

I asked what the differences were in the middle school system between now, since the introduction of the Four Modernizations policy, and previous years; I got quite a lengthy answer. The three years of junior middle school have remained the same, but the two years of senior middle school are being added to by one year. The students have "less control." The students work harder now "because they don't have to go to the country-side to work." And the students are "quiet" in order to pursue the three aims of sound morals, solid knowledge and "fit health."

In the afternoon the model kindergarten was *model* with a vengeance. The Seven Star Kindergarten has 167 kids between the ages of three and a half and six. There are 36 teachers and 16 classes.

A contingent of little girls wearing makeup and tutus, singing and waving plastic flowers greeted us, and we were rushed inside to see a show — songs and gym-nastics — all performed on a wool rug that must have cost a thousand yuan.

We saw an impressively clean set of classrooms and sleeping areas: wooden cribs in rows, tiny quilts folded at the foot of each bed, the children's neatly-pressed clothes in boxes on the wall. In each classroom we visited, the kids jumped up, eager to perform a song for us. The teachers beamed.

This is a kindergarten to which the children go five and a half days a week, arriving on Monday and leaving Saturday afternoon. The parents pay 15 yuan (about $10) a month, which seemed expensive in contrast to, say, our beginning teachers' salaries of 40 yuan a month. But then we were reminded that the parents would have very few other costs for their children, with them away so much. We found out that many of the parents of these children are cadres.

DIARY ENTRY
Thursday, September 18
Shanghai

I have fallen in love with Shanghai. Partly because I have the sense that things here are organized in a more familiar way. I gape at very reasonable facsimiles of Western life, like the tall buildings along the Bund, the bakeries that sell baguettes and French pastries, the sumptuousness of the hotel we're staying in (it is like so many hotels in France that I was never able to afford), the advertising — billboards in English (something we had never seen before in China) and the obviously central role that shopping and consuming play in people's lives here.

Many of these things, of course, are remnants of the old Treaty Port days when China had to pay for her war defeats during the nineteenth century by allowing "foreign concessions" to be set up in her port cities by French, British, German and American business interests. Shanghai became notorious for its foreign concessions, areas of the city where foreign residents were granted immunity from Chinese law, and which often had enclosed sections prohibited to the Chinese. These continental remnants are now part of everyday life in Shanghai — people tear into a bakery on their way to work, pay for Western-looking sweet buns, and eat them at the bus stop or as they hurry along the street to work.

Of course we have been well prepared for this visit by Cheng Qilong, Ian's student, who tutored us in Chinese. He's a native *Shanghairen* (literally, "Shanghai person"), and for months has been telling us how wonderful a city it is. Twelve million people in one city, whew. This may just be romanticism, but there seems to be a cordial warmth in the air between people; the city is very alive. We couldn't believe our good fortune when he told us he would be in Shanghai visiting his family at the same time we were coming. Hearing his voice on the telephone today was not only the ideal welcome to this city, but it reminded us that we could do things, like talk to friends on the phone, that we could never do in Chengdu.

We met Cheng Qilong down at the front gate of our hotel, in order to make sure he wouldn't have any trouble getting in, and we pumped each other's hands vigourously, grinning at the sight of each other.

"What happened to you?" he asked, pointing to our very Western outfits.

"Oh," we laughed, and Ian explained, "we thought we'd better start dressing like *waiguo ren!*"

"You look different, too," I said.

"Oh, yes," he answered. "When I arrived in Shanghai, I pressed my shirts. People dress more carefully here."

Cheng Qilong correctly guessed that we'd want to do a lot of shopping in Shanghai, and he volunteered to take us to Nanjing Road, the main shopping area. He also had a special sight he wanted us to see.

"I'll have to take you down to the waterfront, after dark."

"What for?" we asked.

"That's where you can see a lot of young couples hugging and kissing in the dark," he explained.

"Hugging and kissing in China!" cried Ian in mock prudery.

"I'll bring my camera and flash unit," I promised.

And indeed, that is what we did, minus camera, that evening; it was quite a sight. There were hundreds of couples leaning against the concrete wall overlooking the water, lined up in a long row; and despite the crowding, each couple was oblivious to all the others. We passed a young man, who unlike everyone else, was alone, sitting on the wall.

"You know what he's doing?" asked Cheng Qilong, smiling.

"No, what?" we asked, curious.

"Saving a space for when his girlfriend arrives."

What conclusions can be drawn about sexuality from a sight like this? First of all, seeing any kind of open affection between the sexes in China is a big event, and I suppose that's why we were taken to see this nightly occurrence on the Bund. And if open expressions of heterosexual affection are rare, except in a "sophisticated" city like Shanghai, expressions of affection between gays and lesbians are non-existent. In fact, the Chinese, when asked about gayness or lesbianism, state flatly that it simply doesn't exist here.

Westerners often conclude from the rarity of these instances of affection, or the rigidity of these answers about gayness and lesbianism, that China is a very sexually repressive society; "de-sensualized" is one term I've heard used. These kinds of conclusions I find annoying, for a couple of reasons: one is that I don't think there is a long tradition in China of open sexual expression between the sexes, and that the kinds of taboos that exist around this question have deep cultural roots. The other reason is that Westerners so often identify as sensual only what occurs between the sexes, and have a blind spot about our own culture, with its strong prohibitions against public physical expressions of warmth, particularly between men. I am constantly astounded at how much touching goes on in Chinese society — much more than in our own. The male students in my class would lean all over each other during breaks as they asked me questions or shared their newspapers; groups of three or four young men, university students, would walk along with their arms slung around each others' shoulders; women often walk hand in hand or arm in arm with each other; Miss Li would often stroke my hair, or take my hand, as she talked to me. And the interaction with children is incredibly warm and open.

韓珠

DIARY ENTRY
Friday, September 19
Shanghai

This morning, when Ian and I walked into the opulent dining room of our hotel, the Jin Jiang, we spotted the American journalist, Bill Sexton, we had met in Chengdu. We joined him for breakfast and had an extremely pleasant chat exchanging observations on all the schools we have visited. I expressed curiosity about the differences between the "key" and "model" institutions that we were shown and the "common" schools. He had visited a number of schools and found that the routine and little ceremonies in each were exactly the same as in the model schools he'd visited. "What you see in the model schools," he said, "is essentially how the Chinese educational system really does operate."

He also told us about a few spots to check out, one of them being the large villa-like private club across the street from this hotel. This place, he said, was where Mao spent a lot of time at the beginning of the Cultural Revolution. He recommended eating there. So Ian and I strolled over to see about the hours, and found a big sign outside the door, giving just such information in English. It also warned that "persons with mental disorders" would not be admitted. Ian and I turned and walked away. "That lets us out," we observed.

Again today, we spent the day with Cheng Qilong doing what Ian calls "lightning shopping" all over the city. Today's only concession to the culture, history and politics of this country was our brief visit to the site of the founding of the Communist Party of China (1921). On our way there, I commented to Cheng Qilong about the abundance of displays of mooncakes in the store windows, and about how happy that made me. "Yes," he replied, "you know, now we have advertising on the radio, and these days, many shops are advertising their mooncakes that way." "What?" I cried. "Advertising on the radio — don't you think that's just a little bit too capitalist for China?" He smiled, because he knew I was teasing, and said, "Well, I must say, I was surprised too. It's new since I was here last year."

Ian and I had been nagging Cheng Qilong to take us to the big department store in Shanghai, and I think he was looking forward to the spectacle of our shopping there. One minor purchase I wanted to make was toothpaste, so the three of us wandered around the main floor till we found some counters displaying a lot of tubes of it. I told Cheng Qilong that I couldn't possibly make a decision about which kind to buy, and asked him which brand he usually bought. He couldn't see it, so engaged the salesclerk in conversation; he then reported to me that this was a *special* display of toothpaste, and the regular brands of toothpaste were a couple of counters away.

"A special display" I asked. "What do you mean?"

"Well, all these kinds of toothpaste are from one province, from Heilongjiang, so I don't really know any of these brands."

"I can't believe it," I said. "there must be at least 30 kinds of toothpaste here. All from that one province?"

"I'll show you the kind I usually buy, at the other counter," he offered. I accepted this suggestion, grateful for some way out of this dilemma. I speculated to Ian about coming upon a huge display of Albertan toothpaste in the main floor of Eaton's, and we both agreed this was a curiously surreal form of production, even to our consumer-oriented minds. I then selected Cheng Qilong's brand, made in Shanghai, from an equally large display.

We had two fabulous meals today, both of them with Cheng Qilong. For lunch he took us to a restaurant that was extremely busy with overseas Chinese. We sat in one of the many little rooms on the second floor, sharing our table with some Hong Kong Chinese. The three of us feasted on about 15 Shanghai crabs, which I have to declare the most delicious food I have ever tasted in my life. Our second big meal was at a Western, in fact, French restaurant called Hong Fang, The Red House; our

American journalist acquaintance had told us about it. We had wine, of course, and fish, steak and fried prawns — but all served in that peculiar Western way where each person gets a different dish and stabs at it with those heavy metal utensils.

DIARY ENTRY
Saturday, September 20
Beijing

Through some slip-up, we were greeted by a French-speaking guide at the airport. Mlle Liu deposited us at the Friendship Hotel, a huge foreigners' complex that houses many of the experts in Beijing; it was built in the Fifties, originally for Soviet technicians. It is, unfortunately, located very far from downtown, but the little apartment we were given was pleasant.

While we were settling in, Li Xingui came to tell us that, through channels unfathomable to me, he had heard that our student Zhu Fan would be coming to the hotel in the morning to spend the day with us. Delightful news.

During a banquet held for us that night by the Ministry of Education, I couldn't help noticing how much more practised the Beijing leaders were at making small talk than had been the equivalent members of officialdom in Sichuan. I suppose they are much more frequently called on to entertain foreigners; in Sichuan, it seemed like whole hours would pass at banquets without a word being addressed to us, and our attempts to follow the Chinese conversation swirling around us would go largely unrewarded. At one point tonight, the director looked me in the eye and asked me what had been the most difficult thing to get used to in Chengdu. A tough question, but before I realized it, I had replied: "The noise." Everyone laughed; it may not have been exactly what they had been expecting to hear, but they knew what I meant.

韓珠

DIARY ENTRY
Sunday, September 21
Beijing

Today we were taken by car down to Tienanmen Square to see Mao's corpse in the Memorial Hall there. There were a lot of Chinese people lined up, four abreast ("it's the rule") in the square, and another embarrassing privilege was bestowed on the distinguished foreign guests — we were ushered into line well ahead of everyone else. I asked why, if there was so much anti-Mao sentiment, all those people were eager to see Mao's corpse. Our two companions explained that they must have been people from out of town who were doing it just because it's something to do in Beijing. Not a thoroughly satisfactory answer. The men in line removed their hats as we all mounted the steps leading into the Memorial Hall, and everyone fell silent. I began to comment on this, but Li Xingui admonished me for talking, and Zhu Fan declared all the formality "ridiculous."

Mao's familiar but overly pink face, at rest in an open coffin, showed none of the ravages from the problems in temperature control that had been encountered when the Memorial Hall was first built. One friend of mine, who has made several trips to China as an interpreter, told me that he had seen Mao's face a different shade (once red, once purple) on the two occasions he'd visited the mausoleum. Perhaps I have been seasoned by a Catholic youth, but this open coffin didn't strike me as any more disquieting than the corpses I have seen in many funeral parlours. Mao's public laying to rest is supposedly against his wishes: he had asked to be cremated.

After a visit to the Summer Palace, there was an hour or so before a farewell party at the Canadian Embassy for the retiring Canadian ambassador. We spent it looking over the goods at the Beijing Hotel. We were thunder-struck by the modern department-store appearance of the counters in the lobby. But this culture shock was soon far outstripped by the party at the Embassy. Going to that party was like opening a door and finding myself in one of my aunt's homes in suburban Toronto. Ian and I could only gape at the things that we hadn't seen for so many months: we picked up paper plates and plastic forks and served ourselves from the buffet — chili con carne, potato salad, shepherd's pie, cupcakes for dessert. It was all so bewilderingly familiar, and Ian and I kept gauchely muttering to each other things like, "My heavens! There are paper towels!" Ian was nearly delirious with contentment at finding Campari available at the bar — it was the lack of this very drink that caused him so much mental anguish in Chengdu. And I held onto my gin and tonic the way a child holds onto a teddy bear that she fears some older bully might tear out of her hand.

We took a taxi back to the Friendship Hotel shaken, but safe in the knowledge of exactly what re-entry shock was going to feel like.

韓琳

September 21
Dear Mom and Dad,

I thought I would write one last ceremonial letter from this Republic's capital before I leave, even though it might arrive after I do. We heard there was a work-to-rule or something with the Canadian post office when we were in Shanghai — a wonderful city, the New York of China — so you've probably been feeling isolated.

Shanghai, as I said, was magnificent; we just didn't have the time to do it justice. And the same for Beijing — it's very big and sprawling with wide avenues and so many cars. We've done all the touristy things — the Mao Memorial, the Great Hall of the People, the Forbidden City, the Summer Palace — and tomorrow, the Great

Wall. I would dearly love to have my bicycle; I'm itching to get to know this city.

Well, the last letter. The long haul is almost over. The only thing I'm worried about now is getting through Customs. I hope I don't have to spend the winter in jail paying for my extravagance.

韓琳

DIARY ENTRY
Monday, September 22
Beijing

Ian and I were suffering E Mei flashbacks today, puffing up the Great Wall; it was no easy climb, but, really, compared to E Mei, it was a piece of mooncake. There's just a small trudge from the parking lot till you find yourself on the Wall, at which point you can go to the left or the right. We took the less-travelled path, the left of course, and soon came to the end of the restored part, where from a sort of turret, the crumbled wall stretched for miles. I could then understand how it would be possible for the peasants of the area to cart off bits of the Wall and use them in building bridges and pigsties, as has been reported in the Western press.

We stopped at the Ming Tombs before we got to the Great Wall, and I uneasily recalled some of the things that had been said the day we visited the Mao Memorial Hall. The emperors, too, had been carefully entombed and each province of the country called on to select some of its finest workmanship and natural resources in creating a fitting spectacle for the emperors. Where does the traditional form of respect leave off and unnecessarily extravagant homage begin? I reluctantly began to see the point that some of my students had been making all summer.

On our return in the late afternoon, Ian and I, like cranky children, insisted on going to a *jaozi* restaurant that we had read about in the American Embassy guide to

Beijing (we needed a dumpling fix). Such a peculiar restaurant; booths like a North American restaurant's. We invited our very nice driver for the day; he accepted. However, as the place began to fill up with *waiguo ren*, both he and Li Xingui hastily finished what was on the table and rushed off to wait in the car, leaving Ian and me to have the food that hadn't arrived yet. We felt concerned and wondered why they were uncomfortable at the presence of so many foreigners.

DIARY ENTRY
Tuesday, September 23
Beijing

Every time Ian and I find ourselves with a spare hour or two, we do some last-minute shopping, thinking we've got to bring back some really special gifts from China. The effort is beginning to wear us out. We met a young American couple in a handicrafts store — we'd seen them the day before in the Friendship Store — and we got to talking about this ridiculous shopping.

"I feel as if all I've been doing is consume, consume, consume," said Ian.

"Oh, I see," said the man. "You're consummated."

We spent an hour or so in the remains of Liulichang, a shopping area that used to have lots of antique, curio and art stores. Now these are all rubble, and big *waibin* malls, to attract foreign currency, are being built. The foreign community here sighs at this decision, and expresses the wish that the Chinese would realize that foreigners like the rundown, seedy old crammed shops better than the glossy new kind.

Since we were quite close to his place, we called up our Australian friend, Tony Walker, who had been through Chengdu on a journalists' trip to Lhasa. The apartments in this foreigners' complex for diplomats and journalists are extraordinarily luxurious and spacious, sumptuous in contrast to any living quarters we have seen in China. The possibilities of luxury open to the press and the diplomats in Beijing make life here something less than the "hardship post" it is supposed to be.

Tonight was mid-autumn Moon Festival, the night that we had so carefully been preparing ourselves for with excessive consumption of mooncakes. Strict observation of this festival requires drinking long into the night under the full moon; we complied, but did our drinking indoors, in the bar of the Beijing Hotel. Some of the people who joined us were interested in moving the festivities to a boat in Lake Kunming, at the Summer Palace; that would have been a splendid place from which to view the moon, but Ian and I had packing to do. And so ended our last night in China.

韓珠

DIARY ENTRY
Wednesday, September 24
Beijing

The long-awaited, long-dreaded day of departure. We loaded our suitcases into a Chinese taxi for the last time and got to the airport in plenty of time.

And then began the most amazing bureaucratic foul-up I had experienced in China. We checked our baggage, got our boarding passes for our Japan Airlines flight to Tokyo, exchanged our little remaining sums of Chinese money and sat down in the lounge to spend our last half hour with Li Xingui. Finally, twenty minutes to go, Ian insisted that we board the plane, so with a thousand feelings, we said our goodbyes and went through the Chinese control, tickets and passes ready.

Or tried to. Old China hands, we have since discovered, are perfectly familiar with the necessity of having an exit permit in order to leave China. We weren't. It usually takes forty-eight hours to get one, and there we were, twenty minutes before departure without one.

Useless feelings of why hadn't the Ministry of Education told us, why hadn't the people at the Embassy told us? A huge, furious argument was raging between Li Xingui and the airport authorities, who were adamant that we couldn't board the plane without an exit permit; the Japanese airline steward was looking on nervously, and minutes were ticking by. Ian placed a panicked call to the Canadian Embassy, and spoke to a sympathetic but ineffectual officer there: "You know," said this Canadian, "you can't get anything done in China in fifteen minutes." He had no suggestions.

The argument behind us suddenly died and all the Chinese officials, including Li Xingui, disappeared into some back rooms, leaving Ian and me and the Japanese steward looking at each other desperately. The flight departure time came and went; our disbelief at our plight grew and grew. We could only deduce that the plane was being held until some resolution was reached.

Finally, about fifteen minutes after takeoff time, all the Chinese officials emerged from the back corridors, with Li Xingui in the lead, waving our passports. He pressed them into our hands, hurriedly explaining that a high official at the airport had signed the exit permits after some frantic phone calls and arguing, and he waved us off, shaking his head in incredulous relief. *"Tamen lai!"* ("They're coming!") called the Japanese steward to the people waiting at the door of the plane, and, as Ian and I fell self-consciously into our seats, the plane started up.

And then, a few hours later, as the plane neared Tokyo in the evening, the Japanese man sitting in our window seat beside me made his only attempt at interaction with us. He gestured to me solemnly, indicating that I should look out the window. This meant a lot of stretching and contorting, and I ended up with my head nearly in his lap before I could see what he was pointing to. It was the largest and most beautiful full moon I have ever seen in my life, and I thought it was a very peaceful final note on which to end the hectic challenges of our stay in China.

Bonavia, David. *The Chinese*. New York: Lippincott and Crowell, 1980.

Brugger, Bill. *China Since the 'Gang of Four.'* Totowa, N.J.: Croom, Helm, Barnes and Noble, 1980.

------------. *China: Liberation and Transformation, 1942 - 1962*. Totowa, N.J.: Croom, Helm, Barnes and Noble, 1981.

------------. *China: Radicalism to Revisionism, 1962 - 1979*. Totowa, N.J.: Croom, Helm, Barnes and Noble, 1981.

Bulletin of the Atomic Scientists. *China after the Cultural Revolution*. New York: Vintage, 1970.

Bynner, David, trans. *The Jade Mountain: A Chinese Anthology*. New York: Vintage, 1929.

Chen, Yuan-Tsung. *The Dragon's Village*. Harmondsworth: Penguin, 1980.

Coye, Molly Joe and Livingston, John, eds. *China Yesterday and Today*. New York: Bantam, 1975.

Davis A.R., ed. *The Penguin Book of Chinese Verse*. Harmondsworth: Penguin, 1962.

Endicott, Stephen. *James G. Endicott: Rebel Out of China*. Toronto: University of Toronto Press, 1980.

Fitzgerald, C.P. *Mao Tse-Tung and China*. Harmondsworth: Penguin, 1976.

Fraser, John. *The Chinese: Portrait of a People*. Toronto: Collins, 1980.

Frolic, B. Michael. *Mao's People: Sixteen Portraits of Life in Revolutionary China*. Cambridge, Mass.: Harvard University Press, 1980.

Han Suyin. *The Crippled Tree*. London: Jonathon Cape, 1965.

------------. *A Mortal Flower*. London: Jonathon Cape, 1966.

------------. *Birdless Summer*. London: Jonathon Cape, 1968.

Hinton, William. *Fanshen: A Documentary of Revolution in a Chinese Village*. New York: Vintage, 1966.

Hong Yung Lee. *The Politics of the Chinese Cultural Revolution: A Case Study*. Berkeley: University of California Press, 1979.

Horn, Joshua S. *Away With All Pests — An English Surgeon in People's China: 1954-1969*. New York, Monthly Review Press, 1969.

Kingston, Maxine Hong. *The Woman Warrior*. New York: Random House, 1975.

------------. *China Men*. New York: Ballantine, 1977.

Leys, Simon. *Chinese Shadows*. Harmondsworth: Penguin, 1974.

------------. *Broken Images*. Translated by Steve Cox. London: Allison and Busby, 1979.

915.1

915.1

Lu Hsun. *Old Tales Retold*. Peking: Foreign Languages Press, 1972.

Macciocchi, Maria Antonietta. *Daily Life in Revolutionary China*. New York: Monthly Review Press, 1972.

Mao Tse-Tung. *Selected Works*. Peking: Foreign Languages Press (in five volumes).

Meisner, Maurice. *Mao's China: A History of the People's Republic*. New York: Collier MacMillan, 1977.

Migot, Andre. *Tibetan Marches*. London: Rupert Hart-Davis, 1955.

Milton, David; Milton, Nancy and Franz Schurmann. *The China Reader: People's China*. New York: Vintage, 1974.

Myrdal, Jan. *Report from a Chinese Village*. New York: Signet, 1966.

------------ and Gun Kessel. *China: The Revolution Continued*. New York: Pantheon, 1970.

Oxnam, Robert B. and Richard C. Bush. *China Briefing, 1980*. Published in cooperation with the China Council of the Asian Society. Boulder, Colorado: Westview Press, 1980.

Schell, Orville. *"Watch Out for the Foreign Guests!"* New York: Pantheon, 1980.

Schell, Orville and Franz Shurmann. *The China Reader: Imperial China*. New York: Random House, 1967.

------------. *The China Reader: Republican China*. New York: Random House, 1967.

------------. *The China Reader: Communist China*. New York: Random House, 1966.

Schwarcz, Vera. "Ruminations of a Feminist in China." *Quest*, Volume 5, Number 3, 1981.

Seybolt, Peter J. *The Rustication of Urban Youth in China: A Social Experiment*. A China Book Project. White Plains, N.Y.: M.E. Sharpe, 1975.

Sidel, Ruth. *Women and Child Care in China*. New York: Penguin, 1973.

Smedley, Agnes. *Portraits of Chinese Women in Revolution*. Edited by Jan and Steve MacKinnon. New York: The Feminist Press, 1976.

Snow, Edgar. *Red Star Over China*. New York: Random House, 1938.

------------. *The Long Revolution*. New York: Random House, 1972.

Back cover photo by Carolyn Egan